20 Percent Marketing

...maybe that's all you need

by Paul Holland

ISBN 978-0-9722059-1-7
Published by:
SWG Marketing LLC   Little Falls, NJ
20 Percent Marketing ©copyright 2002 by Paul Holland
all rights reserved

This book is dedicated to the 20%,
you know who you are…

Forward

You will notice in the course of this book that a great deal of significance is attached to goals, so it is only fair that I begin by sharing some of mine.

Obviously the sale of this book generates revenue, for which I make no apologies. Quite the contrary, I am capitalist and proud of the fact. I could never fathom any system that punishes creativity, industry and initiative.

I have attended many classes/seminars and read many books (both good and bad) on the subjects of sales and marketing. There always seemed to be something lacking. They would generally take one of two directions. They would cover theory and cite case studies of industry giants that while interesting were not in a format applicable to a small company —or— they would provide tips, techniques and gimmicks that sound cool but lack substance and become threadbare very quickly.

I recently had the refreshing experience of working with a number of new entrepreneurs. On average 80% of start-ups do not survive year one – 80% of the balance won't survive through year five. Although capable of doing a good job in providing their products and services, one of their greatest challenges is finding and retaining the customers to do it for. As a result, I could not help but wonder how many were reading the same books, attending the same seminars and running down the same blind alleys I had. Then I thought, what if I could create a better path?

20 Percent Marketing grew out of my belief that in life it is always best to be the second man through the minefield.

This is an attempt to take some of my insights and experiences gathered over the course of decades in the field and to isolate the core components that comprise all successful programs, regardless of the size, industry or state of the company. To help define those elemental truths that are consistent in our rapidly changing world.

20 Percent Marketing is meant to aid these small and mid-size companies, the people who cannot afford a marketing program and cannot afford not to have one. It is to help them gain a maximum amount of benefit from a minimum input of resources.

It is also an opportunity for those in the field to take a step back and re-focus on where their best value is coming from.

It is intentionally small enough to travel on an airplane or bus. Hopefully it contains enough information, common sense and humor to make it readable and applicable in your daily life.

I hope you enjoy it and find it profitable.

TABLE OF CONTENTS

Forward

Table of Contents

Appendix

20% Recap

The Golden Rules of 20% Marketing

References and Suggested Authors

Section 1 - Why 20 Percent?

Exploding a Myth.

When I was a much younger man living in a world of vacuum tubes, carbon paper and slide rules - I remember people telling me, "Holland, go into the leisure industry. That's where the real money will be. Why with all these labor saving devices that are being invented, people won't know what to do with themselves."

Today we eat lunch at our desks, the forty-hour workweek is a dinosaur and we hope that we can still make it to the dry cleaner on our way home from the office before he closes at 8 o'clock. What happened?

Technology didn't give us time. It gave us speed and then only selectively. We can move, store and sort prodigious amounts of data in seconds. Documents are whisked halfway around the world in nanoseconds. The average high school calculator has more computing power than the Apollo spacecraft did when it landed men on the moon.

Look at the achievements just in the past fifty years. In 1964, I remember going to the World's Fair in New York. At the ATT pavilion, the biggest attractions were kiosks having two phones side by side. One was a push button, the other was a rotary dial and visitors could try both to see how much faster the future of telephone communication would be. Technology has provided us with some incredible advancements and without our noticing it has exacted a terrible price.

How could we have more powerful tools then ever before and less time? It is because the capacity to make a decision still rests within the human mind. We are the bottleneck. Where we once had three potential vendors we now have thousands. Confronted with this virtually endless array of choices, just like their desktop computers - people freeze up. Decisions are "by committee" in order to defray personal risk, because we are still governed by fear. We spend hours sorting and sifting, just trying to make sense of it all while that false sensation of speed simply aggravates the feeling that we are slipping farther and farther behind.

Years ago the state of technology was such that patience was an integral part of society. You had to wait for a television to warm up. Documents had to be re-typed. Drawings were something done on a board with a tee-square and pencil.

Today we live in a world governed by the click of a mouse and as a result deferred gratification has gone the way of the dodo. How often have you seen see folks verbally and physically abusing a simple fax machine because it couldn't produce a sheet of paper fast enough? By the way, do people still use fax machines? People wonder where road rage came from. It is simple. Waiting 30 seconds at a traffic light has become an eternity. The subliminal message that is reinforced by every microwave meal and movie on demand is that waiting equals being left behind.

Okay then, what's the solution...

In the absence of time and buried beneath an avalanche of options, decisions must be based more and more on relationships. Who can I trust to take this off my plate and not drop it? It is the ultimate means to minimize risk in a decision and regain time BUT if technology isolates us – where do the relationships come from?

2

Be careful what you wish for.

We asked for time…

but instead technology gave us speed…

We asked for solutions...

but instead technology created more choices...

and today we sit at the bottleneck,

just

trying

to

get

done.

20% says, time is the new currency -
and your account is overdrawn...

3

a predictable imbalance...

The Pareto Principle
- 80 / 20 rule -

Vilfredo Pareto lived from 1848 to 1923 and is best remembered for his 80/20 rule. Simply stated, 80% of any result is due to 20% of the input and it is simply astonishing just how often this relationship repeats itself. 20% of the people do 80% of the work, 80% of your profit comes from 20% of your product line, 80% of your problems come from 20% of your clients and of course 20% of your efforts will yield 80% of your return…

The actual amounts will vary to a degree but almost invariably these ratios hold true. We've all seen it time and again.

Here's where it gets interesting…

Let's rephrase it - that means we spend the majority of our time with very little to show for it. How much of our day, every day is spent on minutia, battling a tempest in a teacup.

The real trick is determining which 20% represents your core value, so that you can take care of it first without the distractions of the other 80% that always seem so important at the time.

That's really what 20% marketing is about, locating your core value in any activity and taking care of it first.

Change is the new equilibrium.

Some companies and individuals make the mistake of thinking that their business will return to normal.

Surprise, this is normal. Heraclitus (540-480BC) said, "Nothing endures but change." Today it has been estimated that the sum total of human knowledge now doubles every thirty years and that rate is accelerating.

Change will be a constant companion and every entrepreneur should cheer. Change has always been the harbinger of opportunity. Consider for a moment that the status quo is in fact the mortal enemy of enterprise. Stability by its very definition suppresses anything new.

Change demands new horizons. It seeks to expand the boundaries and push the limits, always.

Many years ago I served in the Navy and when I first went to sea it was difficult to just to stand or walk on a constantly moving deck. After a short while though, it became second nature. You found your sea legs. That's really what we are talking about here. It not so much about seeing the future as it is about creating it. It is not about seeing what technology does but rather what it enables. When we look only at what something does, it fixes us in the present. When we look at the ripple effects things create, we find portals into the possible.

20% looks for what if, not for what is.

Proactive people create their own destiny. Everyone else just wishes they had bought the stock way back when...

It is ironic that technology, by giving us more and more choices, is driving us back to what is tried and true. Too many options decrease the likelihood of our selecting any of them.

In any decision, people will seek to limit risk first and that is exactly what a brand does.

Brand loyalty isn't dying. It is just that the water has become increasingly muddied so it is harder to see them. That isn't the fault of the brand, people want them. They are willing to pay a premium for them, even in hard economic times. When a brand is compromised it is usually because management has allowed it to happen. If you want people to identify with something - it has to be something they want to identify with. A brand must be a point of stability in order to succeed. They succeed because they are anchor points in a stormy sea of change.

20% says brands and relationships offset change and risk.

Remember however all motion is relative. In this day and age of headlong change, you can be left far behind simply by standing still. Your brand has a life. Stable does not mean static. The stability of your brand is rooted in its core value. As long as that promise of performance remains true, aspects that are peripheral may morph and change as long as the do not go contrary to nature of the brand. In fact they often have to in order to mirror changing times.

That is why I am a proponent of the Harry Truman School of decision making. When in doubt I make a decision. If I'm wrong I can always make another one. I have made bad ones and good ones and taken credit for both.

One constant remains.

*Human nature is the one great constant
...and it is governed by relationships.*

The most sophisticated of today's scientific instruments has its roots in that first flint knife. For all its incredible promise, technology is still only a collection of tools.

Despite our outward trappings, people are still people. We love, hate, fear, hope, wish and dream. The primary forces that shaped our ends thousands of years ago are effectively unchanged.

In this constantly shifting world, most people don't like change. They fear it, resist it and to help combat it they will seek relationships as a point of stability. Which brings us to my definition of 20% marketing.

What is 20% Marketing?

20% Marketing is about establishing and keeping a culture of relationships based on your most profitable activities...

It's really very simple, but then you should expect 20% to be just that. It's about positioning yourself to win by helping others to win as well. It is about playing to our strengths, knowing our limitations and defining our actions accordingly.

It's about the best of both worlds. The opportunity brought on by change and the natural stability and channels created by human nature. What could be better - and what better way to secure the future for your company than by marketing accordingly?

Why marketing programs under-perform?

There are a number of reasons, but all have to do with having our focus diverted. The 80% that creeps in to sap our attention away from what is truly important.

lack of identity
>What unique characteristics give you a competitive advantage and how do you frame this from the standpoint of customer perceived benefits?

lack of direction
>Where is the well-defined target, the goal and how will success be measured so we know when we've arrived? Efficiency follows the shortest path.

lack of consistency
>Marketing isn't a sprint - it's a marathon and as in any long distance race, success belongs to the one who sets and keeps a solid pace.

lack of commitment
>Taking an ad, exhibiting at a tradeshow or doing a mailing isn't marketing, they are different tasks that are part of a mix. Marketing isn't a job function; it is a frame of mind - a continuous process that can't be switched on and off like a light bulb. Random starting, stopping & changing simply wastes time & money, it is self-defeating and diffuses the focus we hope to create.

20% says if something does not contribute to reaching the objective, lose it.

20% Marketing Re-Occurring Elements.

Trust - Trust is the backbone of every brand. It influences every decision we make. After all, trust is the basis of every relationship. We willingly pay a premium for a brand because we have confidence in its ability to perform as promised.

Time - Time is the new currency and your account is overdrawn. People will spend money to gain time, even in hard economies, because they are short staffed and wait until the last minute...

Communication - There are four parts to successful communication. These are the target, the message, the media and the benefit of action. Like the four legs of a table, when one comes up short things generally get very unstable.

Relationships - All relationships are based on an understanding and desire to act in each other's interest. Both sides have to recognize benefit. The trick comes in understanding where the other party places value.

People - In doing trend analysis, demographic profiles and reach and impact studies - it's easy to forget that it's really all about people. Companies don't buy stuff, groups don't buy stuff - people buy stuff.

Business - Because results are often deferred or not readily apparent, we forget sometimes that the point of marketing is to provide a return. Marketing for the sake of marketing is just an interesting academic exercise.

The goal here is to concentrate on those aspects that will provide us with a maximum return for a minimum input.

We have all read numerous books and articles detailing hosts of different business models and case studies. Although interesting, any direct correlation to your needs was probably small. The reality is that to truly find value in how IBM solves a problem, you need to be IBM - or - you need to look at them from a different standpoint.

When I was younger I used to dabble with magic as a hobby. It was a lot of fun and it taught me a valuable lesson about problem solving. People watch a magician and they are amazed. They ask themselves "how did he do that" and they have no idea.

To know how the trick is done you need to think like the magician, instead of thinking like the audience. Ask yourself, if this is the effect I wish to create - how would I do it? You are usually not far off in the answer.

Don't look for the ways other companies "do it". Look instead for these elements to reappear throughout this book, other books, articles, your job, other companies, life in general - time and again.

Because that's where 20% is...

"…This above all, to thine own self be true
and it must follow as the day the night
thou canst not be false to any man."
W. Shakespeare, "Hamlet", act 1 scene 3

Section 2 - Finding Core Value...

What is your Credo?

...as a company? ...as a marketing function?

One of the best examples of a corporate credo is that of the Johnson & Johnson Company. It is often held up as a model at business schools. The employees of that firm refer to it not as a mission statement, but rather as a living document.

If you have never had the opportunity, read it sometime.

The word "responsibility" appears five times, the word "fair" four times.

It uses words such as dignity, mindful, privileged and ethical.

It doesn't say anything about global domination or market leadership. Yet they currently have 197 operating companies in 175 countries when last I looked. They employ over 100,000 people worldwide and have been one of Wall Street's most consistent performers.

When you talk about your corporate culture, it is often what you don't say that speaks the loudest.

Write your credo and then live it. The farther you stray from it the farther you get from 20%.

20% says - don't tell me, show me.

Matrix of Business:

	MAINTAIN	MILK
BEST	**I**	**II**
CHEAP	**III**	**IV**

Over 20 years ago, in an effort to explain the cultures of different companies that I dealt with, I began evolving my "Matrix of Business" and was surprised to find that everything fit within this simple format. Some companies would always seek to acquire "the best" - the best people, customers and equipment. Everything has to be cutting-edge, state-of-the-art and then they would do one of two things with them. They take care of their investment (Quadrant I) in ways such as building relationships, training their people and maintaining infrastructure on a regular basis. Their initial acquisition cost is high, but amortized over an extended period. Their retention cost is low and predictable.

Their counterparts (Quadrant II) would begin the same way and then milk the value without maintaining it. Then they usually wonder why equipment fails, employees depart and clients leave for greener pastures.

Their on-going high cost of acquisition is onerous. They are still trying to acquire the best - but doing little or nothing to keep it.

Then you have organizations that inhabit Quadrants III & IV who buy in on the cheap. Where's the least expensive drill press on the market? Who can we hire for less money to perform that task? Where can we get a used computer? Cut the price to buy the business. Sound familiar?

They do one of two things. They try to maintain something by pouring more money and effort into it than it was worth in the first place. They extend even longer discounts to clients who were less profitable when they had to buy the business in the first place. They make do with the computer crashes, lost production time, disgruntled workers and reduced quality. These are the companies in Quadrant III. Although acquisition is low, their cost of retention is extremely high.

Their counterparts (Quadrant IV) simply cut things off when they reach a point of diminishing return and buy again on the cheap. They have a predictable ongoing cost of acquisition and very low retention costs.

Do these sound like companies your know. Does one of these sound like you. We all float to a certain degree between these quadrants but our culture, our attitude remains primarily centered in one of these four areas and there is a point to this.

Invariably people in Quadrants II & III go out of business and often it is not mercifully swift. Companies in Quadrants I & IV make money, but those in Quadrant I are usually the most successful long term.

The reason for the success of Quadrant I and IV style companies is that they are focused on where their 20% value lies. One is concerned with an investment style philosophy, where to put their resources for long term gain. The other assumes a more short-term strategy and maximizes value by simply watching and cutting off the less productive 80% as it appears.

The value in Quadrant I relates primarily to their people and how they interface with their customer base. Frankly, anyone with the time and money can duplicate your physical infrastructure. They can buy the same computers, take the same size ads, go to the same tradeshows, and clone your products right down to the last wing nut. A Company's competitive advantage will invariably rest in the ingenuity and industry of its workforce. Quadrant I organizations build an environment where the best people can thrive.

What is your company culture like?

What kind of cultures do you see in your customers?

Your first best chance in marketing your product or service is to seek out customers with a shared core value system. Let's face it if you are dedicated to being the low cost provider, you are not going to work well with a company that demands premier service. They may have come in for a low price but very soon they begin making demands you can't meet. Or the reverse happens, you are dedicated to a high degree of after sale service but times were tough and you gave up more than you should have on price just to get the work from someone who only values the low cost provider. You wind up doing more, for less profit for a client that doesn't appreciate it. In either case - welcome to Quadrant III.

Unless your culture is clearly defined, you will drift farther and farther from 20%.

Always try to be brutally honest about your company. Others will be (especially customers). Everyone and everything has three faces. What we see, what others see and the reality that lies somewhere in between. In establishing where we are and what we can achieve, we can stop over reaching ourselves. We work more efficiently staying within our abilities and playing to our strengths.

Try a quick self-audit -

Ask yourself these three questions:

- In an acquisition decision (hiring, purchasing, accepting an order, etc.) what factor is most important? What is it that makes you say, Yes?

- In any decision to terminate something (supply agreements, employment, equipment, etc.) where is your cut-off, your point of diminishing return? At what point do you say No?

- How often do you take an order and wish you had not?

If the answers trouble you, that's good. You are starting to find where 80% is eating away at your profitability.

"They denied that wishes were horses,
      They denied that pigs had wings,
            So we worshipped the Gods of the Marketplace
            that promised these beautiful things…"

from "The Gods of the Copybook Headings"
                        by Rudyard Kipling

Section 3 - Are You My Client…

Who is your BEST customer?

Its important to note that it is often not your biggest customer. We all have those clients. The ones who bring us 38% of our revenue (and consume 48% of our resources). This is really about your best customers, the ones responsible for 10% of your revenue while using 2% of your resources. You know, the ones where you appreciate each other's needs and capabilities, where you aren't always putting out fires. *The ones you should clone!*

Write down the top 10…

What do they have in common?
What makes them culturally a good fit?
What do they define as the value in dealing with you?

That in essence helps to define both them and you… Almost invariably there is a shared core value system. Performing this exercise identifies your relative strengths and weaknesses. Not merely what you do well, but what you as an organization believe in. You are the low cost provider and they are price point conscious. They are JIT focused and you never miss a ship date. They need a lot of handholding in implementation and you are committed to after sale service.

People who tell me that in the end it all comes down to price have relegated themselves to commodity status. They are in quadrants III & IV. If that were true why do generic products that cost up to 45% less only hold 20% of store shelves? There can only ever be one low cost provider in any market.

So why isn't every one else out of business? Price is important represents only one part of the equation that makes up value.

The most expensive product or service that anyone can buy is one that doesn't accomplish its intended purpose. If you need a screwdriver, you would not buy a hammer simply because it cost less.

Now write down the bottom 10...
Do not base the selection decision of these customers on their payment history. That is usually most people's inclination. If everything else is right, terms can be resolved. Look instead for where are we just square pegs force fit in round holes. What do these situations have in common and where is their resolution? For example: If the greatest conflict is the time required for delivery, there are two options. The obvious one is to "fix delivery" until we start to look at all that implies. Do you hire more people, increase overtime (and overhead)? Do you outsource work (diminishing profitability)? Do we bump production schedules so that we can satisfy a few clients (at the expense of others)? That's usually what we wind up trying to do.

What if we court and keep customers that do not place emphasis on getting the product at 8:30 the next morning?

Concentrate on getting and retaining those customers where we have the highest probability of success. Clients who value most what we do well and place less emphasis on areas where we know we are weaker. No one can be all things to all people, but matching core capabilities means you can be the best possible option to some of them.

A Few Thoughts About Demographics...

The study of demographics is simply about segmenting your audience along shared characteristics, such as age, gender, ethnicity, income, job title, etc.

This is an area where people new to marketing will sometimes feel uncomfortable. After all, in any other setting defining and grouping individuals along such lines would be labeled as racist, sexist and anything else the politically correct would deem appropriate. (Mea Culpa, I've never been very PC.)

The difference here is that bias seeks to build walls. Marketing builds bridges. We identify groups to better understand them and serve them, not to segregate them. Granted it is for commercial gain (even on the part of not-for-profits), however understanding is the foundation for all sound relationships and anything that decreases the distance between us eventually must benefit society at large.

Some will complain that different groups are unfairly targeted or under-served. Absolutely, but not for very long. Earlier in the book we talked about opportunity. As segments become saturated, competition weeds itself out and invariably the entities that do the best job of appreciating and meeting their needs will win. Other segments are under-served, but only until satisfying that demand becomes economically viable. Once that happens good marketing rushes to fill that void. This is where opportunity hides and where good marketers wait and watch.

20% says look beyond trends at what they imply.

It all comes down to the great color barrier - green.

Where does economic empowerment lie? It is interesting to note that many of the "traditional" segments have lost focus in lieu of a new model. Large portions of the economy now route through hands you might not expect, such as teenagers who control billions of dollars that are virtually 100% discretionary.

80% marketers tend to group people and then look to see where the buying influences are.

20% marketers come to the realization that people will group themselves and instead they follow the money first, then look to see who really holds the purse strings.

Economic empowerment should be the first litmus test. Look at the McDonald's Corporation. Mom and Dad were the ones who drove into the parking lot. They would have to pay for the burgers and french fries, but it was the kids screaming in the backseat that wielded the economic clout. Thirty years ago McDonalds marketed directly and almost exclusively to children. They flipped hamburgers but they sold fun. It was a Happy Meal® world. In recent times they have tried to modify that image with adult menu products and themes to match (Ronald is still around mind you) but with less than stellar results. They looked at trends and moved away from their core business. They thought they were a restaurant. In reality, the food was secondary. They were clean and consistent and the kids were happy. They just forgot.

To be my customer, you don't have to earn the money. You don't even have to physically have the money. You simply need to be in the position to dictate how it will be spent.

We deal in a world of statistics and as a result sometimes it's easy to forget that hidden in those figures are real people. Its like Patrick McGooan's famous line from old television show The Prisoner "I am not a number, I am a free man." I still remember that someone on the sound track started laughing at that point.

Psychographics takes this process a step farther by examining the preferences and attitudes exhibited by different groups. Perception is reality and therein lies the great pitfall in all this.

There have been many times when I've had a client in the B2B sector explain their business to me and I always ask if the final decision maker is an owner or an employee. I cannot recall a single instance when I wasn't greeted by a look of confusion or surprise. That's the type of thing that most people don't think of and yet one is spending their own money, the other is spending someone else's. Same industry, same product or service, same price tag, yet that one fact can have a radically different influence on how they perceive the relative benefits of "the deal".

20% marketing asks first who controls the sale and then, what controls them

And Now A Word About Competition...

More on the order of a few thoughts actually...

First: Any business professional can rattle off chapter and verse, giving you a complete list their competitors. Relative size, share, offerings, pricing and discount policies, an entire list of interesting facts that really don't have very much to do with their real position in the market place.

20% marketing says to truly understand your competitor, become their customer.

If practical, buy something from them. Even where it isn't possible to do that - put yourself through the entire purchase and ownership cycle. From start to finish, find out what their customer experience is.

The objective is NOT to do a point by point comparison, if you even can. You are not the same company nor should you want to be. The goal is to see where the differences are and to gauge the overall experience exactly as a potential client would. Your subjective impressions will be more important than your objective appraisal. For two reasons, customers for the most part do not do a point by point analysis and in this situation your objectivity would be suspect. The important question is where do they obviously place value. If it happens to be in the same general area that you focus in, then the arena in which you compete narrows. If they ship in half the time that you do but you have much superior technical support you really don't compete after all. Your legitimate customer base is one that is less concerned about having it here tomorrow but demands world class service... get it?

Second: Consider the era in which we live. Time is at a premium everywhere. Communication technology has made it easier than ever to "get the word out". As a result organizations of every type and description are locked in a huge shouting match, competing for every eye and every ear. We are bombarded by thousands of messages and images every day trying to command our attention. The problem is compounded by the myriad array of choices that clutter both our personal and professional lives.

Couple this with the trend to down size (or is it right size?) in business today that invariably has people inheriting multiple tasks. You may be selling metal working machinery, only to find out that the person you need to speak with is too busy reviewing accounting software packages to give you an audience. Your competition is anything that steals your customer's attention. AOL founder Steve Case was once asked who his biggest competitor was. He replied, "Nice weather."

20% says your real competitor is the increasing clutter of messaging and the diminishing time to sort through it.

Third: In the immortal words of Pogo, " We have met the enemy, and he is us." We are our own worst competitors. How often do we promise more than we can reasonably deliver? Far more often than we would probably like to admit. Every organization should put themselves through the same scrutiny that was described for their "traditional" competition.

Buy from yourself. Put yourself through exactly what you would put a client through, anonymously of course. See first hand what your customer experience is like. It is usually very enlightening.

Remember that section in which discussed defining our corporate culture. It is an invaluable exercise. This is really where the rubber meets the road. How we perform is the true indicator of what we believe.

When is the last time you called your own technical support people and sought their help as one of your customers would?

When did you last fill out a reader service card or drop a dummy inquiry in among your tradeshow leads to test the efficiency of your fulfillment process?

How often do you track an order from initial contact to completion or critically review your Internet presence?

Don't tell me, show me.

This is the simplest and least expensive form of quality control for your brand. It is performance based, you are experiencing what you put your clients and prospects through. It can be easily instituted and administrated either internally or through an outside agency. It establishes a baseline against which you and other companies can be measured. It is readily repeatable. The most difficult aspect of this in doing it internally is your level of detachment. You have to be willing to truly be the client.

There is no such thing as a dissatisfied customer. There are only ex-customers. Yet we as we deviate from our core capabilities we establish a pattern for failure. It's like walking out onto a lake that hasn't quite frozen solid to retrieve something. As we first venture out we keep telling ourselves that we'll be fine. The footing still seems safe but as we go farther we feel things beginning to shift and crack underfoot.

In business as we move from the security of our competitive strengths "to get the business" invariably we make promises that we really are not certain we can back up with actions. It will be all right; we're confidant that it will work out. That's because we really want the order. The greater our desire to secure that business, the more ready we are to discount the associated risks and make unsupported promises. That is simply human nature.

Please do not misunderstand my intent here. One of the greatest strengths of the entrepreneur lies in their ability to accept risks that other corporate cultures avoid and stretch the envelope with new and creative solutions. In assessing risk, however there is one element that often seems to be forgotten. That is the danger of the dissatisfied customer. Your most effective sales force is your client base. If they are happy with you, they promote you. If they are unhappy with you, well…

When you are calculating risk - reputation is a very odd variable. When adding, it is incremental. When subtracting, it is geometric in proportion. No one tells just on person how unhappy they are.

20% marketing says your biggest competitor is a level of expectation you cannot satisfy.

Successful marketing is in part the art of creating and managing expectations. That is what relationships are built on.

"A person who sets out
    with no particular destination in mind,
    always gets there..."
                    ~unknown~

Section 4 - Start at the End...

They Invented Poker Chips To Know Who Won...

I am always amazed at how many companies fail to establish clear-cut goals for different aspects of their marketing programs and a means to measure them. Granted there are areas that are more difficult to access such as reach and impact, but there are methods that can and must be employed to gauge results. Even relatively simple mechanisms can provide a level of guidance. Whether it's a tradeshow, a print ad or a direct mail piece - without some degree of expectation and a means to measure the outcome you are flying blind.

On May 25, 1961 John F, Kennedy made his famous speech expressing the intent to land a man on the moon within that decade. This was less than 58 years after Orville and Wilbur Wright had changed the course of history. It was only 20 days after the Alan Shepard had taken his place as the first American to reach space, a sub-orbital flight that lasted only 15 minutes and 28 seconds.

In 1969, a scant 8 years later we heard Armstrong's message from our closest neighbor in space, a journey spanning over half a million miles.

In the 1950's space exploration was little more than Buck Rogers and popcorn at the Saturday matinee. In the wake of that speech, every American suddenly owned stock in a dream. After a few trips to the moon, people lost interest for years. It was all still space exploration, but there was no longer a line in the sand. There was no visible goal to keep things focused.

Tracking success basically consists of three elements...
Defining what the goal is in real terms, fixing parameters around it and establishing the means of measurement.

A good goal must pass these tests...

Quantifiable-
Have objective or subjective standards defined the goal? Beware of descriptive language, those insidious adjectives such as better or greater.

Measurable-
What standards are to be used to determine relative success or failure? You must be able to attach hard numbers to performance. Not just sales or profitability, but elements such as reach and impact.

Specific-
Tell me exactly what constitutes a goal. You need to be able to hold it in your hands. Black and white only - there should be no gray areas.

Time sensitive-
Establishing a timeframe is essential. *When* is every bit as important as exactly what or how much.

Attainable with difficulty-
A goal that is impractical from a standpoint of available resources is simply a recipe for failure. Good goals are based on core capabilities and allocated resources as well as current and projected market conditions. Similarly, goals that are achieved too easily discourage effort and initiative.

"Lots of sales leads" is not a goal. Tell me that we want to identify and qualify a potential client base in the Southwest US such that we can meet an objective of generating $400,000 in sales for a new product at a 38% gross margin within the first 12 months - that's a goal.

20% says if it fails to meet these criteria, it's not a goal...

What are your goals for today?
What are your goals in reading this book?

If you don't have an answer, you don't have a goal.

In Dale Carnegie's famous book, "How to Win Friends and Influence People" he relates the story of Charles Schwab, the steel maker. He was the General Manager of The Braddock Steel Works. As the day crew was going off shift, Schwab walked into the changing house and asked how many heats they had poured that day. "Four" came the reply. So Schwab produced a piece of chalk from his pocket and drew a large "4" in the center of the room. Later the night crew was puzzled as they came in and asked its significance. The next morning as the day crew entered to find that the "4" had been replaced by a "6" and the race was on.

Carnegie uses the story to illustrate the role of competition in our lives. It is far simpler than that - it begins with a written goal. That's why they keep record books, so there is something just barely out of reach. Goals are the spurs of greatness but they only work when employed. Write them down and keep them in front of you.

What are your goals in marketing?

Is it to acquire customers or keep them?
Is it to raise capital or awareness?
Often an activity will serve multiple purposes but be clear.
What is your primary reason for something?
That is where 20% resides.

There are lots of good reasons to market, but 20% cannot exist in the absence of written, measurable goals

Hippocrates said, "That which is used develops, that which is not used wastes away." Just like everything else, the more you do it, the easier it gets and the best time to begin a practice is now.

What are your goals - personal or professional? Start writing them down now to visualize them and give them form.

- If you focus only on the present, you react.

- If you focus only on the future, you dream.

- If you focus on a point in the future and draw a path from the present to reach it, you guide.

My Goals:

Do they pass the litmus test?

41

"What's in a name? That which we call a rose
by any other name would smell as sweet."
W. Shakespeare, "Romeo and Juliet", act 2 scene 2

It may smell the same, but it is harder to sell.

Section 5 - Brand and Image...

These terms are constantly held up as marketing icons but what do they really mean, at least from the standpoint of 20% marketing? Here are some definitions that work, Beginning with:

Image - a perceived set of values.
What is the first thing a client or prospect will associate with when they hear your name? Your image is not what you see. It is not even what you project. Your image really exists within the minds of your audience.

What do you want them to associate with your company?

How would you describe your company?
___ Conservative
___ Professional
___ Contemporary
___ Progressive
___ Family - Friendly
___ Leading Edge
___ High Tech

How would your clients describe your company?
___ Conservative
___ Professional
___ Contemporary
___ Progressive
___ Family - Friendly
___ Leading Edge
___ High Tech

You have the ability to influence that but your control is limited. Mark Twain said that, "no man has a good enough memory to be a successful liar." People and organizations get into trouble when they try to spin an image that their core value system cannot support. There is no foundation for it and eventually it will topple. Look to see how broad the discrepancy is between how you view yourself and how your customers see you. That will tell you in a hurry if you are on solid ground. Companies will fool themselves by believing they must live up to something they are not and shouldn't be.

At one point in time many years ago, I had two customers that both manufactured mailing machines. One was a market leader. They were dedicated to pushing the envelope (no pun intended) through technical sophistication and superiority. Ironically, the actual mechanical functioning of the majority their equipment up until that time had not changed in over 50 years. It was basically about picking up paper and putting it in envelope.

The second company saw an opportunity. They simply took apart a 50 year-old machine and started manufacturing a clone. There were no bells and whistles. Obviously their machine could not match the functionality of its state-of-the-art rival but it sold for a fraction of the price. As a result they carved out a profitable niche piece of business. Had they tried to adopt a me-too mantle and chased that elusive cutting-edge posture, they would have failed. They remained true to their identity of no-frills, just-basic performance and did very well.

20% does not waste the resources to prop up something that cannot stand by itself.

Now lets move on to the other half of this section and begin with the definition of:

Brand - performance insurance.
In his book, *The Invisible Touch,* Harry Beckwith makes an interesting point. He claims that the brand is not owned by an organization, but by the consumer it serves. Companies may own the trademark. They may be able to sell a brand as a tangible asset but it belongs to those consumers who adopt it as their own. I think it goes one step further. A brand truly succeeds when the user abdicates part of their identity to it. They are incomplete without it. When Coca-Cola introduced "New Coke" an amazing thing happened. The new product was both a dismal failure and a rousing success. From a new product introduction standpoint it was a dreadful mistake, yet it was exactly what the Coca-Cola brand needed to re-invigorate itself. The faithful rushed to the product's defense. Sales of "The Real Thing" skyrocketed. Has anyone seen a bottle of New Coke recently? By the way, for an insider's view read Sergio Zyman's book, *The end of marketing, as we know it.*

The real lessons here are simple. First, people don't drink Coke because they are thirsty. If that were all there was to it, they would simply drink water or anything close at hand.

Second, a brand is like a public park. You water it, weed it, sweep away litter and keep the paths clear - that makes it an open and inviting space. What make it a park are the people who come and build memories there.

What would make people attach such loyalty? Once I was watching the holiday classic film "A Christmas Carol" with my children and I remarked that Scrooge was a very foolish man. They asked me why and I replied that he loved something that couldn't love him back. In this life everything is purchased with the same currency. If you want a material thing, you buy it with money. You acquire respect by respecting others. You make friends by being a friend, and so on. If you want people to be faithful to a brand - it must be faithful to them. It must always perform exactly as promised. People are willing to pay a premium for a brand because it saves decision time by reducing risk.

Branding requires four elements:

Consistency
> Trust is the currency that is used to purchase brand loyalty. We trust what we know. There must be a sense of familiarity - predictable and recognizable elements in consistent settings.

Clarity
> People inherently distrust that which is vague - to make your message reassuring, make it clear and concise. Remember, nobody has time, deliver Identity, Purpose & Value in 2 seconds or less.

Repetition
> People forget and everything competes for their attention. You need to constantly remind them and reassure them that your brand is there and steadfast.

Change
> That which never changes becomes background noise. Recast the familiar elements of your brand in fresh packaging to keep it front and center.

20% knows that everyone has a brand; some just manage it better than others do.

Good or bad, reputations follow you. If your product or service performs erratically or inconsistently that is precisely what people will trust it to do.

Brand management is expectation management. Putting yourself in a position where you can consistently and reliably perform and then reinforcing that impression in the mind of the target audience.

Name One Thing In Your Job That Doesn't Matter...

Then I guess it all matters...

The reality is that there is no neutral ground when it comes to your image and your brand.   If no one has time and everyone is continually bombarded by messaging, then everything you do either contributes or detracts. Every day we employ letters, sales presentations, phone scripts, packages, faxes and everything that touches the client touches the brand. Since you must use all of these, use them to advantage.

20% employs every tool more than once.

Thomas Jefferson said, "The price of liberty is eternal vigilance." ...that is also the price of your brand.

"No one after lighting a lamp puts it under the bushel basket, but on the lamp stand, and it gives light to all in the house."
Matthew 5:15

Section 6 - Spreading the word...

There is an old adage that if you invent a better mousetrap, the world will beat a path to your door. I believe that the person who said that starved to death.

The Sony BetaMax was a better product than VHS tape, but VHS won. The Apple computer was faster, simpler and more stable than the PC platform, but PC won. The Tucker automobile was years ahead of its time. I believe there is a shopping mall now on the original factory site.

Great products and services pass into extinction every day because the people that could benefit from them the most were not aware of their existence at the right time. The benefits were not clear. They lacked identity.

Communications and marketing are joined at the hip and successful communication is built in four steps. Your identity has to be broadcast morning and night - AM PM.

A   Audience— who is it going out to?

M   Message— what is the content?

P   Pay-off— what is the call to action and its benefit?

M   Medium— what media channels will you use?

Like the four legs of a table, take any one out and the whole process falls down.

20% says good marketing beats good products and services.

Audience

You can sell to the wrong person all day long—but they are not going to buy anything.

Lists and database management are critical components of any successful direct marketing program. The choices are simple. You can develop them in house or you can access them via an outside group or agency.

The first best choice is to develop them internally. A well maintained list is a tangible asset. It can be sold, rented or shared. In the sale or transfer of a business it is often one of your most valuable properties, but frankly it is not a very glamorous job. Face it, not too many kids collect database manager trading cards. It is unfortunate because it is the backbone of the entire process. Common areas for prime list development are through existing customers, associations, tradeshows and networking events because they inherently pre-qualify candidates.

New ventures generally suffer from the lack of a well functioning list but then so do many well-established companies. It is not quantity - it is quality that matters. When someone says that they have 50,000 contacts in their lists, the next question should be "How many buy anything or have real potential to buy anything in the future?" If all you want are names, pick any phonebook.

The Constitution not withstanding, not all clients are created equal. The whole idea behind building a profile of your ideal customer is to clone them. Don't build one list; build several using different criteria that are important to your objectives such as current purchasing status, preferences or potential.

The information contained in lists is often invalid. Make sure that lists are current and de-duped to minimize sending out multiple and incorrect messages. As an example, in a recent survey by CEIR, the Center for Exhibit Industry Research, they found that 30% of tradeshow leads contained typographical errors. Your lists are like a garden, requiring constant care and weeding by removing or updating erroneous information. In addition, clients move and people change jobs all the time.

Isn't better to send out 5,000 highly targeted direct mail pieces 10 times than a single blast to 50,000 relative unknowns? The cost is the same.

20% says it is about quality, not quantity.

How do you develop internal lists from scratch? The best sources are the ones that have the highest degree of pre-qualification built in. This would include tradeshow and direct sales contacts, call-ins, referrals, and information inquiries from the Internet and other advertising media. There is a subtle but significant difference between "leads" that are typically dumped into commercial databases. The majority of these contacts are really only inquiries for additional information. Their value is limited until they are qualified by telemarketing, sales contact or other survey.

One of my favorite places to construct the "A" list has always been through a periodic survey of the sales force for their top five or ten prospects each. Lists like this constantly rotate and keep your best opportunities in front of you.

Outside agencies can be an excellent source for different projects such a new product introduction. There are a host of different companies that compile and rent lists, in addition to providing various direct marketing support services such as direct mail, telemarketing, broadcast faxing or e-mail.

The principle concern is how current and accurate the list is and whether it is permission-based (opt-in). In later sections of the book detailing different direct marketing methods and mediums, opt-in is discussed in greater detail.

List houses should explain up front what steps they employ to help insure the activity of their product and how it was sourced.   One method being used for list generation today via the Internet relies on programs called spiders. Spider programs scan Internet sites for information that fits specific criteria, such as e-mail, street addresses, telephone and fax numbers. Techniques such as this also have value in their ability to fill gaps in databases where only part of the contact is known.   It is critical to note that obviously any information obtained by such means is NOT opt-in.

Also discuss with any potential vendor their policies with regard to compensation if their list fails to deliver as promised. If they guarantee less than a 2% failure rate on delivery and you experience a 10% failure rate—how will they make good? Who will handle requests to have a name removed and what will that incur? If they are handling the mailing or broadcast, what reporting do they have in place to verify the success rate? When will you receive it and in what format?

20% says know your best customer, including where to reach them.

Messaging:

How can you best present your message in the age of information overload? Narrow it as clearly and concisely as possible in a well-defined hierarchy.

Who you are, what you do and most important - what you can do for the client. Your message must deliver Identity, Purpose and Value in that order and ideally, the first two elements must happen in less than two seconds...

Identity: What's in a name?
I remember sitting and speaking with a client once and during the course of our conversation, he alternately referred to his company both by its name and by its initials until I stopped him. I asked, "What do your clients call you?" His initial reaction was somewhat puzzled, until he realized the reason for the question. They were guilty of breaking the first rule of identity. If you are not consistent about what you call yourself, how can you expect your customers to keep it straight?

Names may be descriptive or not. What is truly important is that they convey a unique identity. Unless your firm has the luxury of being an IBM or ATT with decades of established presence a corporate monogram is not going to do that for you. Company and brand names should be short, no more than 10 characters. They should be memorable and easy to pronounce. Be careful of slang and alternative meanings in other languages, stories such as the Chevrolet Nova are legend. By the way, does your "monogram" have a negative alternative meaning?

20% says your name is a focal point for association, make it good...

Purpose—What do you do?

Taglines are a great tool to rapidly telegraph your purpose, what it is you really do. That presumes of course that it is well constructed. There are companies who must think taglines and mission statements are one and the same. Far from it. A tagline is like a compass setting. It merely indicates a direction. It points to our core values.

A Business of Caring - Cigna
Like A Rock - Chevrolet
Translating Opportunity - Scudder Investments
No Boundaries - Ford
Be All You Can Be - US Army
The Ultimate Driving Machine - BMW
Just Do It - Nike
Easy as Dell - Dell

What do all of these have in common? They are short. Good taglines are typically 5 words or less. They are descriptive and highly visual. They convey benefits to the end user without necessarily defining what that specific benefit is. A good tagline pre-qualifies our ideal customer by proclaiming where we place value and asking if they share that view. Isn't that what we really want?

Nike's tagline, *Just Do It* is so successful because it allows the "It" to be defined by everyone individually. *Easy As Dell* works, because they are dedicated to make sure it is easy.

20% says to be believable, do what you believe in.

What's in it for the customer?
The third level of your messaging hierarchy consists of a brief synopsis of benefits from the consumer's perspective.

What will your product or service do to make their business more profitable and productive? How will it make their lives more satisfying and convenient?

At home in my garage is this machine. Every spring I wheel it outside and put gas and fresh oil in it. I prime it and pull on the start cord a few times (hopefully, only a few). Then it makes a devilish racket and spews exhaust fumes while I pilot it around my yard getting grass stains all over my sneakers.

Although I own a lawn mower, I don't want one. I do however want short grass. Sufficiently that I'm willing to tolerate the drawbacks of owning and using the darn thing.

Most companies sell features but that is not what people buy. I don't care that the mower has a super dual mulching action but I want the benefit of not having to rake. When purchasing the mower the POP signage proudly proclaimed the feature. As the consumer I had to make the intuitive leap to realize I get to play golf sooner. Why not simply sell "golf sooner", save time and increase the probability of success?

What is your short grass?

Most marketers think in terms of getting some one to buy from them. 20% marketers see that their message is really trying to buy time from the client. You are trading benefits for a few precious seconds of their day. To do that some intrinsic value must parallel the goals of the target audience.

Charles Revson was quoted as saying, "In the factory we make cosmetics, but we sell hope."

When you look at your company from the clients' perspective, what comes to mind? Write client-focused core benefit statements based on your 3 key benefits. Consider the 80/20 rule in generating ones that are central to your capabilities. What are the value points that provide you with a unique, competitive advantage?

What business are you really in?

You make canoes, but people buy a fun day at the lake.

You make work boots, but people buy feet that are safe and don't hurt at the end of a long day.

You provide landscaping services, but people buy envious neighbors.

20% marketing says your real business is determined by what they buy.

Never telegraph more than 3 key benefits at a time.

The purchaser is usually attracted to the one aspect that holds the most value to them. They won't remember the balance and it will only cloud the issue. This is the age of information overload. Don't add unnecessarily to it. It is a question of balance. Remember that 20% of your benefits will account for 80% of your sales but they will not remember 80% of what you tell them.

Keep it tight.

The myth - less is more, *is wrong.*

We've all seen those glib and creative advertisements. Entertaining showcases that leave the viewer wondering what the point is. I once recall watching a Super Bowl half time commercial for a dot com company which featured an elderly gentleman and a chimp sitting outside of a garage. After 30 seconds, they proudly announced that they had just wasted $2,000,000. Fortunately I did not own stock in this company, although I'm afraid that a great many other people did. I don't think that they are in business any longer.

I am less concerned with winning a Cleo award than I am in meeting objectives. *Clarity is more.* As your message becomes increasing complex or increasingly subtle, the length of time required to process where the benefit is increases and time is that element is in such short supply today.

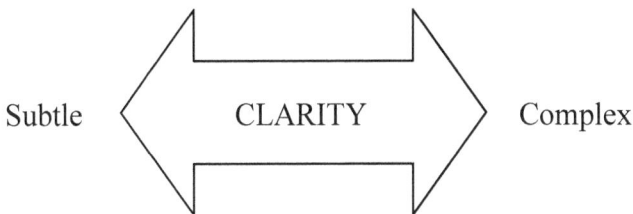

Subtle ◄ CLARITY ► Complex

Consider the 80/20 rule in constructing a set of client focused benefit statements. Different products or services may have their own benefit statements. The same products or services may have different benefit statements designed to address the needs of more than one market. They need to be relevant to both their target audience and current market conditions, but don't roll them together.

That doesn't increase the probability of success, it merely muddies the water. If the customer sees your product as saving them time, why bother to tell them it weighs less, packs smaller, runs faster and jumps higher. If they don't care, you are talking yourself out of the business.

20% tries to match only the key benefits to each specific audience.

Try this simple exercise to help you develop your key benefit statements:

Name the top three reasons why someone should do business with your company and no other and you cannot say price, quality or service unless you can quantify it!

Take a second look; have you named features - or- benefits as seen from the customer's perspective?

What are the three greatest challenges facing the customers you serve?

What are the root causes for these challenges and how do your strengths answer them?

Often you have to go several layers deep to find some of these answers. Your market may be challenged by the inability to hire and keep good people. That is the symptom. The root cause may be their inability to afford health benefits. It may be that they offer no career development path. Perhaps they have a high burn out rate due to stresses. Common symptom, but multiple possible causes -

dig deeper.

Imagery
We do not think in words. The abstract printed characters that litter these pages are reassembled to paint pictures mentally. The ancient Chinese proverb - a picture is worth a thousand words is exactly correct but the pictures are in our heads.

We process images 400 times faster than text. Words are our poor effort to translate and record human emotion. They are important in that they help direct and channel thought but images transcend language and speak directly to the point.

When you visualize the core value system at the heart of your brand, what images come to mind?

Logo -
Try this simple experiment; draw your logo from memory. How difficult was that to do?   How accurate were you? How long did it take you?

Your logo is your corporate signature. It should comprise a unique and immediately recognizable statement. What does your logo say and how long does it take to say it?

Color:
Color and shapes play an important psychological role in telegraphing your message. There are almost as many theories and studies as there are colors, but everyone agrees that they have a strong influence on preference and activity.

In fact, in 1948 Max Luscher devised his famous Color Profile Test. This is a powerful psychological tool, which identifies personality types was based exclusively on the subject's order of preference in selecting of a handful of color sample tiles. It is amazingly accurate.

Here are some general guidelines, ranging from warm to cool:

Reds: energy, excitement, power, passion
Oranges: confidence, friendly, harmony, adventurous
Yellows: wise, playful, optimistic
Greens: healing, heath, rebirth, contentment
Blues: honest. integrity, trust, steadfast
Violets: majesty, mystery, inspiration

Gray and brown hues create stable backgrounds. Although this is often thought of as secondary, this contrast provides a stable platform for your company logo and other elements. On a sheer percentage basis it is the overwhelming predominate color. Take a piece of letterhead—what portion is logo and what is background? Think of how effective the use of background was in the play "Dracula" or Spielburg's movie "Schindler's List" where a single color is introduced against a black and white backdrop.

Because messages must appear in multiple medias, look at how they will reproduce at different sizes, in black and white and grayscale.

Cultural influences:
It's far more than just a language barrier.

Shapes, numbers, colors and positioning can have radically different meanings in other cultures. You may be targeting one group today, but be careful not to exclude future potential markets in the process in creating an identity.

In examining any culture look at the relative influences, these include:

- Language & dialects
- Religion
- History
- Education level
- Work & leisure activities
- Gender disparity
- Independence vs. interdependence
- Ethnic or social division
- Family (nuclear, extended or fragmented)
- Arts & entertainment

...as well as taboos, morals and rituals, where do they place value and blame?

Often influences may not be readily apparent. For example, average literacy rates in a developing country may be skewed by a gender disparity so the rate for men might be considerably higher than that for women. In targeting different groups you need to examine each in terms of all these influences. It is not merely a question of job description and age, but at when did they enter the workforce. An American at 22 may be just starting their pursuit of a paycheck while their counterpart in another country could have 5 or 6 years at their career.

In other cultures alternate education such as apprenticeship or trade schooling are more prevalent. What would be considered a gift in one setting might very well be a bribe in another.

The price of entry is immersion. If you want to earn their business, you must earn their trust and respect. You cannot do that unless you respect their value system.

Many years ago when I was in the Navy, I was walking down a street in Cartagena, Columbia and met another sailor from my ship. He was trying to purchase something from a street vendor. Speaking only English, he was not getting very far. Fortunately I had taken several courses in Spanish and had the opportunity to spend some time in Spain and Latin America, such that I was able to step in and help him get what he wanted (for considerably less than he would have paid - this is a culture that values haggling). I still recall that the fellow looked at me afterwards and said, "It was a good thing you came along, everybody here talks foreign." I stopped him and said, "Look around you. This is their country. YOU talk foreign."

20% does business on the customer's turf and terms.

This section could easily fill libraries. Seek assistance with regard to target market specifics. Your best guidance will come from an experienced consultant here and in-country assistance. In this way you have a check point versed in both cultures and a source immersed in the current scene. Have translations done by native speakers and have them done twice, from English and back again by a second party to see what has changed other than just the words.

The meaning of language only exists in context.

Theme Development

Everyone talks about positioning in marketing and the position that really matters the most is in the customer's long term memory. Once you have established what it is that you need to tell them, how do you make it stick?

To have the greatest influence on human memory, you need to examine the three key areas.

First: We think in terms of association and as a result we remember things in context. My mother was a mezzo-soprano who sang opera, quite beautifully. One day while driving back from a business meeting in Pennsylvania, Leontyne Price came on the radio singing Gershwin's Lullaby. I pulled off the road and stopped the car, closed my eyes and was transported back in time. I was 10 years old again on a lazy August afternoon seated beneath my mother's kitchen window listening to her voice, feeling the sun and the breeze on my face. I called my mother that night to say thank you. That is the power of a theme. It creates a context within which memories form elevating them from events to experiences. That only happens when each of the component parts contribute to the overall effect. The famous architect, Ludwig Mies van der Rohe said, "God is in the details." That is really the point. Anything that does not add - simply distracts and detracts from the end effect. Nothing is neutral.

Rather than viewing each action as just an isolated task, look at how it relates to everything else. A unique concept for a mailer, print ad or graphic might "wow" people and be contrary to the rest of a campaign. It does not mean that it is a bad idea; it is simply not theme appropriate at this time. If it is that good, save it and make use of it when there is a good fit.

Second: Our primary input is visual. It makes sense then that our strongest memories are keyed around visual clues.

Former Basketball Great, Jerry Lucas went on to a second career teaching memory techniques. At one point in time, on a bet he memorized 500 pages of the Manhattan telephone directory and claimed that anyone could do this using his method. Basically this mechanism consisted of mentally building sets of unique, powerful graphic imagery around the material that acted as visual clues.

In developing a theme, based on an understanding of your core values and strengths and the challenges you are answering for your customers, ask what kinds of images come to mind? Core values are invariable abstracts - strength, stability, speed, comfort - seek universal graphic links to express them.

Third: The higher the degree of involvement, the more people will remember in detail. Research in the area of education has long demonstrated the importance of active participation in forming long term memory.

Involvement can be physical, mental and/or emotional. Take the challenge, demo the software, test drive the car, identify with the little kid in the ad - involvement makes us take ownership.

Once we are involved, we begin to visualize benefits and build associations. The incredible volume of sensory input we are subjected to on a daily basis serves to de-sensitize us. We tune it out. It becomes white noise. The best themes change that by creating a single point of connection, a bridge of relevancy that the customer can make their own.

How do you begin to develop a theme?

What are the customers really buying?

What problem or need do you satisfying and who are you solving it for?

Look at the pressures people face today. Whether you work in B2B or B2C environment, a business is simply an extension of the people that make it up. At the end of the day, a purchase decision may be influenced far more by a person's concerns over something like their job security than by any product feature.

20% says the great constant is human nature.

By definition, the best way to develop a theme is by using people. The human mind is the ideal laboratory, because it comes complete with a built in set of preferences, emotions, experiences and perceptions. By employing groups of people we broaden the range of experience and influence. That is why marketing uses things like test markets, focus groups and surveys. The effort is to take subjective responses and put them into objective terms. Whether your firm uses market research or not, invariably theme development comes down to making the creative intuitive leap. GOOD NEWS – you can do that on your own but it takes practice.

Mind-Mapping Techniques - We think and remember via association so what does our core message conjure up? Don't discount anything at first. Write every idea down. Doodle, draw and sketch - we think visually. No matter how absurd something may seem on the surface. In working with a group any idea that is devalued stifles creativity. People are less likely to contribute if they fear rejection and ridicule.

Change perspectives - Work from the other person's position. This artificially builds understanding and broadens our scope of experience.

Weave a tapestry - Starting with these ideas as a nexus, begin weaving a series of scenarios where each might be incorporated into different media and setting. How will salespeople use it? How will it script? How might it fit in a print ad or mailer? How can these images be integrated in different forums to attract your target audience?

Play Devil's Advocate - Will THEY get it, the customers and prospects, or is it too obscure? How does it fit in alternative settings? Does it have any negative connotations or downsides (remember the Chevy Nova)?

The last word on themes is not to trip over our personal baggage. We become enamored by our own solutions, but are we going to buy it? It is not about what you like, or I like - it is about what works. The fact that your favorite color is blue should not have any bearing on what your logo looks like. In the same token, simply because I like the picture of the little kid with the balloon is not the reason to use it in an ad. One of the great inequities of this business is that lots of ideas (good and bad) get placed on the table, only one gets chosen. Sometimes it is not the best one. Sometimes it is a very bad one. When this happens, the reason is simple. Somebody forgot the mission and let their ego get in the way of good judgement. The fact that something is our idea or that it really appeals to us personally is the worst criteria to make a selection by. Most people do not run companies or create ad campaigns - success requires that we think outside the box and put ourselves into the shoes of the average customer in making final decisions.

Does it work across multiple mediums? Is it consistent with our core value structure? Is John Q. Public going to get it, in less than 2 seconds? Those are the litmus tests where 20% hides.

20% says an actor can play to himself, he can play to his critics or he can play to his audience - only the last one actually buys a ticket.

The Pay-Off:

The pay off is a call to action. When we take an ad, attend a trade show or send out a mailing piece - it is to accomplish a particular task. Visit a showroom, clip a coupon, call a toll free number or go to our new web site. There are in reality two pay-offs, yours and the customer's. In addition to your key benefit statements what promotions, premiums or incentives will have the greatest appeal to your target customer? (don't simply assume price)

Discounts
Premiums
Coupons
Demonstrations
Trial Offers
Reward Programs
Option Packages
Contests
Add-Ons
Time or Quantity Limits
Strategic Partner Offers

Get maximum mileage from such activities by making certain that they are appropriate and compliment all other branding efforts. I once had a devil of a time trying to take a large account away from a particular competitor who had enjoyed a virtual monopoly for several years. The crux of the problem was this: our product was technically superior in every way. It consumed less power, ran cooler, easier to mount—the list went on and on. The problem was that our unit sold for about 20% less and people have been conditioned to equate price with quality. After several months, the client finally tried one of our products and called me up. He said, "It does everything you said it would; now explain how it could cost 20% less." I responded, "Why don't you call the other company and ask them how their unit can cost 20% more?" We got their business. The point is the difficulty came from the seeming inconsistency. If it is better, how could it be less money? How often do you see "get the best for less" campaigns?

Look at ways that elements can be blended with different themes to increase consistency and memorability? It generally does not cost any more but when you can make that happen, you get immediate and future benefits.

For example, when you just extend a discount it is momentary. It helps to grab an immediate piece of business but it can also train people when NOT to buy. Just wait, it will go on sale. Isn't that what happens when a discount or a coupon stands by itself without any additional value.

That is because it is not the product or service that is memorable, it is the discount they remember. Make the discount into something that must be earned - become a member, be one of the first 50 to visit the showroom. When you earn things, they have an increased perceived value. The customer becomes an active participant.

Your Payback:
Remember to build in your feedback loop.
"How did you hear about us…?"

Simple mechanisms are easily put in place to help you gauge the affectivity and profitability of each facet of your program. It is just a question of the discipline of listening, recording and analyzing the results across different mediums.

The Medium— your marketing mix:

In Nimes, the Pont du Gard still stands after almost 2000 years. It is a Roman aqueduct rising 155 feet above the river Gard. What is truly interesting is that its three tiers of arches are dry laid stone. No mortar, no cement- simply well crafted blocks each supporting each other for two millennia. That is what a sound marketing mix does for you. Each of the component parts support each other to make something that none could do independently.

Each type of media has their own relative strengths and weaknesses. There is no universal solution. When Avaya first spun off from ATT they had a great advertisement that asked the question, "What is the best way to contact your customers?" The answer was, "Any way they want." There is a great deal of wisdom in that. With all of the furor over the Internet, in the year 2000 only about half of the United States was even on-line. The balance of the globe lags behind that. Does that mean that the web is a bad medium? No, of course not. It simply means that reliance on one or a few media can limit your prospects. Using a sound marketing mix to deliver the message provides three benefits:

It increases the likelihood that any particular medium and target are compatible. John hates the computer but loves getting mail; Mary lives on the web but hates "junk mail". Our message should be able to reach both.

It increases the likelihood that our message reaches them when they are ready. Confronted with the sheer volume of the information dump that takes place on an on-going basis, timing is critical.

Attention spans continue to shrink. They don't need it until they need it and they won't "hear or see it" until then.

It increases overall recognition. The all important, "Yes, I remember seeing that somewhere." Brand recognition lends credibility. The fact that someone has seen or heard of your company, product or service before - even if they don't recall the circumstances of where or when increases the probability of a positive reaction.

In terms of your needs look at different media with regard to it's relative value in customer acquisition, retention and/or brand awareness goals. Shown below is a sampling of the relative rankings of the some common methods used by companies based on one survey by the Direct Marketing Association. Percentages reflect the perceived value of each activity.

Activity	Retention	Acquisition
TV	7%	93%
Radio	10%	90%
Outdoor	16%	84%
Print	24%	76%
Tradeshows	24%	76%
POP display	27%	73%
Direct mail	32%	68%
Telemarketing	37%	63%
Package insert	45%	55%
Catalog	71%	29%

Activities which work well to acquire new customers are not as effective assisting in retention, while methods that are best for retaining clients are generally not as helpful at finding new ones. That should not come as any shock. Acquisition will rely more on timing, placement and immediacy while retention needs residence time.

Budgeting

In creating your budget, you have to work backwards.

If the primary goal is customer acquisition, then your spending in different media is going to reflect that. You are going to rely much more heavily on direct mail than package inserts - on tradeshows than catalogues. If your intention is principally to strengthen relationships with your existing client list and market deeper in existing channels then the opposite is true.

What is your relative cost per thousand (cpm) and more importantly, are they the thousand you are looking for? If it is not the audience you are looking for, no matter what the service is <u>it is a waste of money</u>. If you market exclusively in the Metropolitan New York Area, you wouldn't rent billboard space in New Mexico because it's cheaper. Yet, time and again you will see companies take ads, go to shows, make mailings or engage in other campaigns just because "they were a good buy" or "we always advertise there".

20% marketing says never spend - invest!!!

Budgeting and return on investment are integrally linked or at least they should be. How many times do we take the same ad in the same magazine or make the same mailing to the same list. All to often programs get left on autopilot, but the landscape is continually changing. Every element should be able to justify it's existence based on it's own merits. What has more value? A campaign that produces 5000 inquiries and 200 sales with an aggregate value of $50,000 - or - one that produces only 2000 inquiries but 400 sales with an aggregate value of $120,000. All other factors being equal, most people would choose the latter.

Always eat dessert first. Begin at the end.

It is not about how much it costs to go to the show, place the ad, mail the postcard or air the commercial - it is all about how much it costs per prospect to meet the goal.

20% says the most expensive hammer is the one that doesn't drive nails - regardless of how much it costs.

What is your cost per thousand (cpm) for the medium? (include list rental, sort and deployment costs et al)

What is the scope of the campaign in thousands? (work backwards based on the anticipated response rate - example: goal = 1,000 responses, @ 2% average response rate implies we need a 50,000 list)

What is your total cost for this segment of the mix? (remember that different media and vendors may incur minimum contract sizes, you want to reach 10,000 but they won't write a contract for under 20,000)

Keep a percentage of your budget for contingencies and to capitalize on opportunities. Problems will crop up (and cost money). These media are business entities and just like any other they run special deals periodically. (So ask.)

Most of your expenditures are short term and project specific and budgets are sometimes skewed by a long range or capital expenditure. Amortize rather than direct expense activities where appropriate because they will be used repeatedly such as art acquisition, creative fees or exhibit construction.

In speaking with clients they will bemoan the fact that they spent thousands of dollars for a portable display to attend a trade show. Why, are you throwing it in the nearest dumpster afterwards? Look instead at the effective cost per impression over its life span. It is probably negligible.

Let's say that you spend $5000 for a portable exhibit and it goes to 5 shows a year for 5 years. Do the math. That translates to $200 per show. Wait it gets better. Suppose that each show was attended by an average of 4000 people. That translates to 5 cents for each impression. There are many people who will take exception to these figures because they don't take the cost of use into account. That's the point of this exercise. Yes, there are expenses for shipping, storage, space rental, drayage and more - all valid use costs that are part of each event budget. They are direct expense; the original capital acquisition is not.

Look at the development costs associated logo design or tagline development. That simple symbol and phrase that appear in everything from letterhead to billboard ads, how much do they really cost?

What percentage of this work do you plan on doing in-house and/or out-sourcing? The advent of resources such as desktop publishing and on-demand printing has altered the complexion of what was the traditional purview of agencies. This has lead to a number of creative things and a host of very bad ones. I had at one point in time dealt with a particular client who needed several graphic panels prepared for a tradeshow. They insisted on preparing the art in-house "to save money". To make a very long and painful story short, the production house had to reject the files due to inherent problems several times.

In the end the client wound up paying someone else to prepare the files including rush charges and express freight to get a final product they were unhappy with just to make the show.

There are good reasons to do work in-house, to save money and to use your understanding of the market and your capabilities. There are some good reasons to farm work out, to save time and money (because you are resource constrained) and to augment your industry knowledge. Sometimes we are too close to the problem to see it clearly. We become enamored with a solution not because it is the best one, but because it is our own. That is just bad business. This is not about hiring an agency or a consulting firm. Good budgeting of resources requires a detached and critical eye. Marketing is odd in that it requires both a creative and pragmatic skill set. You are simultaneously both an artist and your harshest critic.

Where is the money actually spent? Different techniques such as mass e-mail and fax can cost pennies, while a well-constructed telemarketing program might run two to three dollars a contact. Direct mail can vary from a simple postcard to high-end targeted promotions that have virtually no upper limit.

Industry surveys rank budget allocation percentages slightly differently but the listing shown on the opposing page by the DMA is indicative of the order in which companies invest in different methods.

The amounts spend are not always indicative of reach. In addition, there is always crossover. Direct mail may promote a tradeshow or a POP display will be used to help distribute catalogs.

1. Direct mail
2. e Mail
3. Events
4. Telephone
5. Search Engine
6. DR Newspapers/Magazines
7. Banner/pop-up ads
8. URL/PURL Campaign

What is noticeably absent is the latest "Hot Button" social networking BUT then something is always evolving. As of this writing 24% of respondents had no idea how much it cost them, 33% spent less than 5% of their budget on social media – yet smaller companies were much more likely to invest up to 50% of their marketing budget here. It is also interesting to note that 2/3rds of those surveyed had no way to measure results.

Reality Check— worry a little more about the cost of looking bad more than the cost of looking good.

Marketing typically expresses budgeting in CPI (cost per impression) or CPM (cost per thousand) but the reality lies in Value Per Impression, how much staying power the message has in the context of the customer's world.

Understanding the customer, their preferences, problems and perceptions allows us to place our solutions before them in a way that they will be most apt to adopt them and make them their own. Since its impossible to know which message will be picked up and when - every piece of mail, every telephone script, every meeting at a tradeshow has the potential to form the basis of a business relationship and should be treated with its appropriate significance.

20% says, there is no perfect mix but there's good enough?

As a starting point in building a sound mix,
lets look briefly at some different techniques...

Section 7 - Media Overview...

But First...

Each of the following is intended as a brief overview of some of the most common mechanisms employed in direct marketing. Frankly each section here has each been the subject of many books in their own right. The purpose is to provide the reader with enough information to determine whether or not it may make a useful addition to your marketing mix. If so, hopefully it will spark more questions than it answers and give you enough background to ask them intelligently. It also points out some of the common pitfalls.

In some areas you will find some discussion of the legal implications involved with different methods. This book is not and should not be construed as a legal guide. There is no reasonable way that this industry snapshot could possibly be complete or current for every venue. New law will be created before the ink on this page is dry.

All advertising and marketing is impacted by many different laws and regulations imposed by federal, state and local jurisdictions. Prudence dictates you get guidance. Contracts, disclaimers, restrictions - what you don't know can hurt you a whole lot.

Print

Print advertising is one of the first media that people think of. It often consumes the majority of the marketing budget because it touches so many areas.

Consider some example:

- Periodicals (general & industry specific)
- Newspapers
- Books
- Catalogs
- Directories
- Packaging
- Sales Literature
- Technical Documentation
- Correspondence

For the first time in 550 years - print is being gradually displaced by electronic media particularly in the areas of sales literature, technical documentation, directories and correspondence.

Desktop publishing and on-demand printing are opening new opportunities to selectively create customer specific catalogs or offerings. Color can be readily and economically used in a variety of media where it was previously impractical. Materials can be personalized like never before in conjunction with database and CRM systems.

There are also creating a number of potential problems by drawing companies in that are new to this environment.

Desktop Publishing Pitfalls

- Acceptable Formats
- Graphic Resolution
- Color Matching
- Media Limitations
- Copyright
- Proof Read

The print world has it's own language and culture that grew up over hundreds of years with moveable type. Today numerous software solutions have been evolved to interface between the computer screen and printing press but success depends on understanding what that transition entails. The print world exists for the most part on a Macintosh platform and most of the business world uses PC's. Compatibility issues are not uncommon. Printers use software designed specifically for the graphics and printing industry such as Quark, Illustrator and InDesign. Always get guidance before sending your material to a printer as to allowable formats. Converting files takes time and time is money. In addition, as a standard practice always include a hardcopy print out of the final layout as you want it to appear. You should also get a proof for sign off and approval prior to production. This is a common practice and a good one. It is a last opportunity to proof read everything. Having paid for print that could not be used due to errors (that I signed off on) this is experience talking.

The work that is created on the computer and output on your inkjet printer will see a degree of color variation when it goes to press. At times the color difference can be dramatic. All color print processes drift. Even when providing a color match such as a PMS (Pantone Matching System) number they are not foolproof.

That simply provides a formula for mixing the ink. The type of stock that it is printed on, the saturation, whether or not it is laminated are just a few of the many different variables that can affect your outcome. It is best always to provide a color proof so that they operator has something to match against. Photographic and lambda processes also color correct. Since these are continuous tone (instead of an applied ink pattern) calibrating the color at one point changes everything else. If you are have large-scale graphics to be produced, ask for a test strip (a portion of the work) to be run on the production equipment for approval.

In the area of graphics one of the most common errors is in the area of resolution. Once an image has been fixed digitally or on photographic film its resolution is limited. There are huge libraries of digital art available for commercial license on the market. When you select images for campaigns, always consider the largest possible size that it will be displayed at. Companies will often acquire art for use in brochures or web sites that is adequate to that task but it cannot "go larger".

After investing in building an identity around these images, they find that they must go back and re-acquire larger files for use in venues like posters, POP or tradeshow displays- if they are even available.

20% says think ahead and buy it once.

Another area for potential difficulty comes from adhering to copyright, trademark and other legal requirements. Only the original artist may copyright their work. You can license its use for different purposes but depending on what those are different fees may apply.

Even "royalty-free" art has limitations on its use. Releases often need to be obtained from owners of properties or subjects in photographs. The manner in which text is worded can have dramatic legal implications. I am not an attorney. The only advice I can or would give to anyone in this area is to get appropriate legal guidance.

Desktop publishing opens a host of choices. I had worked with one company that decided they would save money by preparing their own art for a tradeshow rather than pay for a production artist to assemble and format the material. They had someone on staff that was knowledgeable but there were problems. Files were returned several times due to errors, omissions or corrupted material. Although the person had experience with the software, he did not do this kind of work everyday. In the end, the client wound up paying rush charges to a production artist to rework the job in order to make the show. Could they have done it given more time, probably... Should they have done it, no. Technology only makes things possible. It does not necessarily make them practical. Magazines have closing dates. Tradeshows start with or without you. If you think that an ad is expensive, buy the space and have nothing to put there because of a legal or technical glitch.

20% says core capabilities hold the greatest profit, just because you can do something does not mean you should.

Direct Mail
In one survey commissioned by Pitney Bowes and conducted by Peppers and Rogers, 34% of respondents said that direct mail had the most significant influence on their perceptions of and reactions to companies. They used such adjectives as informed, involved, organized, relaxed, personal and private in describing the aspects of this medium that they appreciated most. 45% said direct mail had inspired some action and 22% said they bought something as a result. 39% went to a web page as a result.

One of the most significant numbers may be that 78% said they appreciated its non-intrusive nature.

Direct mail accounts for one-half of all mail volume, approximately 300,000,000 pieces per day. Yet people feel it is non-intrusive. Unlike many other mediums the recipient is in complete control or so they think.

On the outside
The goal is to always tip the scale in your behalf. Mail can assume many different forms. What would work well to help you stand out in your situation...

Mail is more than just the #10 envelope. Different sizes and colors can help you establish a unique character.

Look at three-dimensional pieces such as tubes, cartons, boxes and sleeves. These will increase cost but can also raise the worth. Interesting shapes and die-cuts and produce a similar effect but everything you send should be capable of processing with automated sorting and canceling machinery or you will pay higher postal fees.

At the other end of the cost scale, self-mailers and postcards have increased in popularity as color-printing prices have decreased on short runs. The self-mailer has the advantage of being it's own envelope and can have impact prior to opening. The postcard delivers its full message, both graphic and text immediately to anyone handling the mail.

One of the most powerful tools in direct mail today is the high degree of personalization that print on demands affords and the good news is that technology has made it increasingly affordable.

Four of the simplest and least expensive ways available to anyone to get a direct mail piece to stand out are:

1. Use an unusual color or size envelope.
2. Hand Stamp rather than using a postal machine and pick out unusual, colorful stamps.
3. Hand address or individually print the envelope. Cheshire labels are easy to use and inexpensive but they depersonalize and cheapen the piece.
4. Show the key benefit or other information on the outside so that it can be seen prior to opening. For example, if you are fulfilling a request for information from a reader service card or tradeshow - say so on the outside. That way the recipient knows immediately that this is not just an unsolicited piece.

Always consider who opens the mail at the customer? If it is routinely a person other than the one for whom your message is intended, you may be getting stopped at the gate.

On the inside
The content must follow the rules of good messaging or it will quickly be heading for the recycling bin. Regardless of the format that the mailer takes, identify and qualify

yourself, state the key benefits to the recipient and your call to action. Everything must defend its existence by supporting the brand - how with this particular mailer contribute?

Repetition can be one of the best tools to help you keep your message alive if there is value and content to support it. Newsletters, industry tips or event schedules are just a few ways to give them a compelling reason to avoid hitting the wastebasket unopened. If people expect that they will always find a benefit in what you send them two things happen. First not only will they open your mailer; they will wait and watch for it. Second, they will equate your name with a value. Like Ed McMahon says, "Watch your mailbox." What do you watch for?

Look at your own mail to see what it is that you open. Periodically, look at the trash to see what is discarded without a second glance. There is that shared culture and relationship thing again. If you and your client base place value on the same things, you will see it in the same places.

20% says, if you wouldn't open it - why would you expect your customer to?

Catalog

Where appropriate - catalogs are excellent tools for both driving sales and promoting brand loyalty. They rank at the top of the list in customer retention for a number of very sound reasons. Catalogs take up residence. People keep them around and refer back to them as resources. They have a strong secondary and tertiary readership. People tend to share them within groups. Catalogs are seen as references, they have an extremely high-perceived value. The advent of selective on-demand printing and CD ROM reproduction allow very highly targeted personalization of catalog content at economical rates.

The most successful models are those which are more than simply listings of products and prices. They combine non-commercial elements to educate, inform and assist their customers. A catalog of camping equipment might include a list of historic trails or camp recipes. Athletic equipment suppliers might have articles on famous moments or obscure trivia in sports. One of my personal favorites has always been Land's End because they would include articles that would often feature different employees at the company. What a simple and elegant way to promote a sense of relationship than by humanizing your people. Suddenly tasks such as purchasing and shipping are not performed by anonymous beings but instead by people with faces and voices and stories to tell. It will be interesting to see what happens to the company in the wake of their recent acquisition by Sears.

20% says customer acquisition happens when you are seen as a source. But customer retention happens when you are seen as a resource.

Most businesses offer more than one just one item or one type of service. What elements of the "catalog" might be advantageous in your business, either alone or in a co-marketing opportunity with a strategic partner?

SHHH... A Note About Privacy

The American people in particular are very concerned about privacy issues. You want as much relevant information as is necessary and practical about your customer but ... You don't necessarily want them to know how much you know...

Television

Television was once the exclusive arena of the wealthy but this is no longer the case. The proliferation of channels on cable and satellite, along with other avenues such as closed circuit transmission have opened a host of opportunities to narrowly target audiences both by area of interest and geographically. This spectrum of choices has the additional benefit of allowing advertisers to craft well defined packages tailored to their needs, including budgetary ones. Exactly what competitive and regulatory forces will do in the future may be subject to speculation, but no one can doubt the power of this medium particularly in client acquisition and brand awareness.

The cost of entry on the production side has plummeted as well due to advances in multimedia technologies. When you consider that the same material can be repurposed for Internet use – it becomes even more affordable. The cost to produce a commercial can now range from under one thousand to hundreds of thousands of dollars. Granted at the low end this may consist of a slideshow and voice over placed in local cable for fifteen-second spot ads. Before anyone sneers, consider this; many of the most effective commercials have been low budget - case in point, Park's Sausage. Do you recall that annoying child that could whine across three octaves? No pyrotechnics, no herding cats, no celebrity endorsements, yet in supermarket surveys people who vowed they would never purchase the product - already had. It was in their cart. Remember it is about business. It is about results.

Do you what to thank the academy, or listen to the cash register ring?

Radio

Radio continues as one of the top rated media for customer acquisition. The average American listened to 967 hours of radio broadcast in 1999, up 3.2% from the previous year and ahead of broadcast television*. It has been projected that listening hours in America will reach 1,012 by the year 2004*.

The Telecommunications Act of 1996 allowed a wave of consolidation in the radio broadcasting. By 1999, 70 % of all stations in the top 168 markets had been merged, many of these into large national chains. The resulting reduction in competition lead to significantly higher advertising rates. Three chains alone accounted for 84.1% of all industry assets in the survey*. Despite these rate increases, continued growth was projected in excess of 12% a year*. On a per ad basis, radio is still significantly less than other media based on projected reach. The principle disadvantage is that it has no residence time. It lacks the strength of a visual input in terms of memorability. Unlike print, as soon as the message is delivered it is gone. The price point can allow many more repeats to help compensate for this.

The medium affords an excellent opportunity to narrowly target different groups geographically as well as based on their demographic and psychographic profiles through the selection of stations serving these segments. Their program format provides a natural selector in the same way that magazine editorial content does. Your placement in time slot will also greatly affect your target audience profile and cost. What programming is it up against? It is as much when they are listening as what they are listening to.

*Veronis & Suhler, 2000

Audio commercials are relatively inexpensive to record, providing you have done your work up front in terms of planning, scripting and rehearsal.

Needless to say, using professional voice talent and/or celebrity endorsements will affect the overall production budget. However, if that is what puts you over the top, amortized across the number of times your ad plays - it can be cheap at the price.

Multimedia

The proliferation of technology has dramatically reduced the cost of entry on very sophisticated methods of portraying your image. It has also spoiled us... We have seen cyber babies break dance and dinosaurs walk after 50 million years - what are you going to do to wow me now?

Obtaining maximum value from any multimedia investment requires planning to amortize its use in as many different media as possible but that is also easier to do. This both provides more value and insures consistency in messaging and image. It just makes good sense both in marketing and economics.

Some of the areas where multimedia has all ready been successfully employed include:

- Internet
- Mobile applications
- e-mail
- CD-ROM
- sales presentations
- tradeshows
- interactive demos
- kiosks
- interactive games
- e-learning & training

Where could you make use of this technology in advancing your program? It is like the old story about the farmer who hires a man to train his mule. The fellow walks up and before saying a work, hits the animal square on the head with a bat. When the farmer protests, the man doing the training replies, "Well first you have to get their attention."

The escalating battle for mind share that rages today continues to stretch the limits of technology and there in lies the problem. Some people make the mistake of enslaving themselves to the "cutting-edge". Unless you are in the business of producing a multimedia based product or service, do you really need or want to be at that level, especially if 20% of the effect might give you 80% of the value? Particularly in this area it is easy to lose sight of the goal at times. Multimedia is like the cherry flavor that they put in cough syrup - it's only purpose is to help the important ingredients taste a little better on the way down. If it does not carry the weight of the message or overshadows it, it is counter-productive.

20% asks, is your message entertaining -
or simply entertainment?

The first purpose of any mar/com program is to advance the business. By educating, informing, stimulating interaction, evoking thought, sharing experience - there are any number of tools today to bring your message to the audience. However, in this era of time compression clear and concise content is critical.

"The medium is the message." Marshall McLuhan, 1964

The last part of that quote today should read, the medium is the message - because if you aren't careful the flash is all that they will take away.

Internet
Currently, over 77% of the United States is on the Internet, and 88% of them have made at least one online purchase. (Although it is growing rapidly, it still only represents 7% of retail sales.) It is really not possible to discuss the Internet without addressing in some fashion the dot com fiasco that knocked the stock market for a loop in its infancy.. It did two things. It proved that the Internet is an incredibly powerful tool and that it is only one tool. The dot crash was not the fault of the Internet; it was people allowing themselves to be blinded by greed. It included a number of poor business plans that no one would have looked at had it not been for Internet fever and unfortunately when they did their high profile tumble they took a lot of other viable businesses with them. (Now I can get off the soapbox.)

According to an article by Creative Good, in a survey of web users conducted in 1999 62% had given up at least once while trying to effect a purchase on-line. 42% of these had turned to traditional channels to place their order and 40% of online job seekers could not apply for a job because of difficulties navigating a web site.

How far have we come? In a survey conducted by eMarketer Magazine in 2001 here are the top 10 complaints by people using the web:
1 - lack of customer service
2 - privacy
3 - higher prices (shipping)
4 - security
5 - confusing architecture
6 - inability to touch, see or feel
7 - lack of trust
8 - inability to return goods
9 - download time
10 - lack of stock

Take another look at these 10 complaints and think about the recurring elements of 20% marketing. All of these relate to trust, saving time and improving communication. Yet almost despite our worst efforts, e-commerce is continuing to grow at an aggressive pace.

The 2000 U.S. census showed that 18.4% of the total value of all manufacturing shipments were transacted over the web. B2B by far out paced all other sectors accounting for 94% of all e-commerce but it is only a question of time before wholesale, retail and service sectors catch up.

The Veronis Suhler Communications Industry Forecast had predicted a 40.7% growth rate for the Internet in 1999. The actual measured growth that year was 73.7%.

Based on industry surveys the firm Ernst & Young has predicted that by 2005, 10 -12% apparel, accessories, toys and 20 - 25% books, music, software, electronics, videos will be purchased on-line.

According to this same 2000 study, holding it back are the disparities of web based commerce-
44% of companies reported different sku's for on-line product offerings.
34% of the companies surveyed had different on-line pricing structures.
89% of shoppers had abandoned at least one shopping cart (primarily due to a price disparity) and 11% of the companies used on-line shipping and handling as a profit center.

If 9 out of 10 people walk out without buying anything - how much of a profit center is that?

How to get the most out of your Internet program -

Surveys so that the majority (46 - 87% depending on the survey) of new web pages are located through search engines.

All search engines function via different and changing algorithms. That's why an identical search conducted using more than one engine will deliver different results and of course most people rely only on one. Most of these tools rely first on META tags and first page content. A META tag is a general listing of keyword content that is not visible to someone visiting the site. Keywords can and should include things such as common misspellings, plurals and terminology.

20% says search engines are always changing - but most web sites are static.

For example, a few years ago a biotechnology company might simply repeat the term "DNA" twenty times in their META tag knowing that a search engine looking for that would be drawn by having that term come up repeatedly and place that site higher in the listings. The level of sophistication has greatly increased. Today engines discount multiples such as that so the same tactic today would work against you. When was the last time you critically reviewed your web site? Here's a hint - your customers critically review it every day…

Ways to improve your performance -

Avoid unnecessary large graphic content, unless it has a specific purpose in delivering your message it can dramatically increase download times.

Watch the use of jargon. The catch phrases, buzzwords and acronyms that different industries commonly employ build walls. Some will argue that the use of such terms demonstrates an industry specific knowledge and that it's absence might be seen as weakness. Here's an alternative that may help. Offer a glossary page where someone new to your industry might go and find out the latest buzz without the embarrassment of having to ask. Wouldn't that increase the likelihood that they will become repeat visitors?

Keep text clear & concise, just as in print - don't talk down to people, but the goal is to do business - not prove the extent of our vocabulary.

Assume your visitors are new to the web and provide easy to use search tools. Simplify navigation (more than 3 clicks and they are gone).

Assume the viewer has a narrow page width (800 x 600) and watch download times (10 seconds @ 28.8 on dial up). We naturally assume that everyone else can access the Internet in the same fashion that we do. There are pockets of the US that still have rotary dial telephone service. So, allow the viewer to skip the cool multimedia intro - have a text option instead. Some will never be able to download it. Others will say that they have seen the cyber baby break dance and they are in a hurry.

A cookie is a bit of code that is installed on the viewer's hard drive when they visit a site. It benefits the user in that when they visit your site again, it has already preserved some kernels of information about their preferences so that they don't have to re-enter data.

The benefit to the site owner should be even more obvious in that it readily permits the ability to track your repeat visitors. If you use cookies, declare them. Privacy statements should be prominently displayed. This is a huge issue on- line and the Big Brother complex is alive and well.

Reports, counters or guest books can all help gauge your ROI.

20% says - No one will complain that your site loads too fast or is too easy to navigate.

Above all - avoid fluff, keep the content relevant and consistent with your branding mission. Be vigilant, within this changing landscape - how hard are you to find?

Chasing technology is great unless it takes you away from your core values.

e-Mail

There are currently over 2.5BB e-mails sent everyday worldwide.

Broadcast e-mail is one of the most effective tools in driving people to a web site. After all they are already on-line. If you have your own list, it is very inexpensive to employ and can be done with relatively common hardware and software. A number of online businesses have grown up to handle deployment.

In different studies done by IMT in 2001, broadcast e-mail has generated about a 1.4% response rate on average.

The single most critical component of a successful e-mail is the subject line. Keep it and all the text clear and concise. The goal is just to elicit another action such as a click through to your web site. Avoid the use of attachments or large file content that will increase download time. Users are justifiably concerned over virus and attachments are much more likely to trigger firewall filters.

Unsolicited e-mail (spam) is generally regarded as an unwanted intrusion and in addition to being viewed as annoying by some customers, spam can carry severe legal penalties. Although it is interesting to note that in a 2001 study done by Ernst & Young, 14% of users accessed a new web site through a URL embedded in an *unsolicited* e-mail, play it straight. Obtain guidance prior to using broadcast e-mail. Many servers and firewalls now include filters to help prevent or limit spamming. Spiders and other methods are used to create lists of addresses without the user's permission. Know the source of any lists that you access. You are ultimately responsible for opt-in compliance, not the list vendor.

caveat emptor

Opt-in e-mail does not have these restrictions. These are lists where the recipients have provided the sender with permission to forward them information. But not all opt-in is created equal – it can get into some very gray areas.

One of the greatest values of e-mail is the speed of response. In two separate studies Jupiter Research reported an 80% response rate and Digital Impact an 85% response rate within 48 hours.

Broadcast Fax
Broadcast faxing is a very common and effective means to reach an audience. Be aware that unsolicited faxing is an illegal practice. Under Federal legislation: Title 47, Chapter 5, Section 227 the practice of sending unsolicited faxes provides for a penalty of at minimum $500 per copy. In addition, local and state regulations may apply as well. Obtain guidance.

After the courier type envelope, faxes are the most widely read printed material. This is an inexpensive media, similar to mass e-mail in cost with certain provisions:

Limit the number of pages sent and the percent coverage. In addition to reducing transmission time the piece will generally be more readable. Ideally transmission time should be under 42 seconds. Most fax machines are relatively slow compared with e-mail transmission.

Use simple fonts, the most important thing is clarity. Keep in mind that this is a black and white medium. Subtle gray scale images may be lost in the process.

Always include a reply action such as a return fax number or toll free service as part of the call for action.

Test a fax piece to see final product as it will appear on the recipient's machine.

Obey opt-in regulations, the penalties can be severe for broadcasting unsolicited faxes. It is a common practice, just like speeding on the highway and just like speeding - people do get caught. Know your list source and provide an opt-out line.

Voice Broadcast and Messaging

Voice messaging is a hybrid between telemarketing and broadcast fax. It is similar to broadcast fax both in terms of cost and affectivity. The process is relatively simple. A scripted voice message is recorded and broadcast via telephone usually to be left in voice mail. The primary purpose of the message is to prompt a particular secondary action such as a return call or web site visit.

30-60 second sound bytes are broadcast and recorded into voicemail with a reply mechanism built in. The reply is typically a toll free number where additional information can be accessed. This may be through an additional longer recorded message, a recorded message with an interactive hierarchy to appropriately direct the call or an inbound telemarketing service if you want or need a personal interface.

Voice messaging may also be used as an inbound interim step to disseminate information to callers that have been prompted by other media such as radio spots, print advertising or direct mail.

Obviously, scripting is crucial. In particular, pay attention to the initial greeting to capture and hold interest.

The Do Not Call list and other regulations apply.

Scripting

After imagery, the spoken word has the single greatest impact on emotional response. We have all seen great public speakers move a crowd.

Scripting has value with regard to all personnel that interface with your customers either over the phone or face-to-face. In some cases scripting is meant to be used verbatim, such as in an outbound telemarketing campaign. It has uses in many other areas to provide general direction and guidance. At tradeshows, in field sales,

Has a salesperson ever over promised to get the order? Has a receptionist ever told some one what they wanted to hear to just to get rid of them? Has a service technician stretched the truth because they felt foolish saying they didn't have the answer to a question at their fingertips?

Scripting is not just something for telemarketing or sales. Anyone that interacts with the customer (and that usually means everyone) has a vested interest in demonstrating a similar level of professionalism. This chain truly is only as strong as the weakest link.

Key areas or points pertaining to your product or service and your ability to supply it such as costs, policies, terms, shipping, delivery, etc. must be controlled or expectations will be created that will not agree with your ability to perform.

Years ago, I knew a salesperson that lost the largest single account his company had for an entire product line. It was not because of anything he did or did not do. It was not because of a competitor. Two engineers met at a conference, one from the company and one from the client. Naturally they struck up a conversation and the customer related his concerns over a "corrosion problem". The difficulty was far more perceived than actual. Failures due to this were a very small percentage. In each case, the difficulty was related to an error by the end user. The engineer from the vendor explained that they could not solve the problem and the customer took their business elsewhere. Sales had no idea that these conversations were taking place. They never had a chance.

Your people have the single greatest effect on long term memory. Scripting is not merely reading from a piece of paper. It is an integral part of creating an identity. It is about not leaving things to chance. Many people also make the error of thinking of scripting in terms of giving out information, when it's greatest value is in obtaining it.

Good scripting includes good questioning. Close-ended questions will only get you a yes or a no (and most of the time it will be a no). Open ended questions that can elicit both facts and impressions. They initiate dialogues, the foundation of all relationships.

Marketing is about relationships after all and relationships are something that we form with people. People who listen.

The old saying in sales is that first they buy <u>you</u>, then they buy the company then they buy the product.

20% says the <u>you</u> is who ever communicates with the customer.

Telemarketing

In the great scheme of societal order, telemarketers would probably not rank very high on many lists - except for those who use their services effectively.

In 1999 industry spent $60BB on telemarketing. They invested this money because it generated $460BB in sales. Interruptions during dinner not withstanding - Telemarketing Works. It ranks very high particularly in the area of customer acquisition. It is important to note that there are two sides to the operation of a call center, outbound and inbound. In this case we are talking about outbound where the telemarketer initiates the call from a list.

There are a great many restrictions that apply to this activity and they will vary due to state and local regulations. Currently, 14 states have Do Not Call lists and other restrictions are active and pending. These include such things as the use of autodialers. The DMA (Direct Marketing Association) maintains a National Do Not Call list that about 85 of suppliers are estimated to adhere to. For obvious reasons, the industry wishes to remain self-regulating.

It is a very hard profession and burn rates tend to be high. If you are choosing a vendor to provide outbound services in particular, look at their attrition rates and average length of employment.

Outbound calling services generally require much larger contracts than do inbound services. Outbound is after all a numbers game. Inbound is primarily for after-market and service support; here opt-in regulations do not apply because customers are initiating the call sequence.

This type of service may field calls for a variety of purposes from order entry, appointment scheduling, information requests or redirecting to other services. Inbound call centers may be used either as a temporary measure for a large time specific promotion, or as an on-going partner to handle a toll-free service line.

Either outbound or inbound, whether you are performing this task in house or using a contract service - scripting is crucial.

If you are using an outside vendor, how do they schedule employees, full-time vs. part time? How and to whom do they route calls? How do they handle Do Not Call requests? Where do lists come from? What formats and reporting do they provide to verify performance? Ask hard questions.

20% says a call center is transparent to your customer - as far as they know, they are talking to you...

Tradeshow & Event
Tradeshow and event marketing is one of (if not the most) complex methods of direct marketing. As a method it is effectively mid-stream, strong both in the areas of customer acquisition and retention.

The power of this media is that it permits you to meet and interact with tour customer base face-to-face, unlike other forms of direct marketing that are one or more levels removed from personal interaction. For this reason, it provides the ability to jumpstart relationship building.

In 1999 approximately 125MM attendees visited tradeshows in North America alone*. In 2000, North America was home to 13185 exhibitions*. Once you include international events these numbers roughly double and the exhibition industry was forecasted to grow at 5.6% per year in 2000**.

Certainly the events of September 11th had a dramatic effect on this venue. Immediately following in the wake of that tragedy, hundreds of events were cancelled or postponed. Due to the interdependence of exhibiting and the need to travel this was reasonable and expected. In the long run, it will also serve to accelerate some trends that were already in place. Shows will shrink in size, as their number will increase, becoming more regional and specialized in nature. The number of attendees will decline but the overall "quality" of leads will improve. The people who go, will be the ones with the most reasons to be there. The intervening period saw a resurgence but current economic turndowns have once again had a dampening effect.

The reason for the resilience of the tradeshow and event venue is that they simultaneously provide answers to two of the most pressing demands of society today.

*CEIR, **Veronis & Suhler

1. Time compression, we can see hundreds of people - vendors, customers, distributors, peers - plus new products and emerging trends in days or even hours.

2. Direct human contact, we are after all social creatures. That is our nature. That's why we built cities. Market day is thousands of years old. Perhaps that's why it costs on average 45% less to close business initiated on the tradeshow floor*.

Why do tradeshow programs under-perform then:

You're at the wrong show - your audience is elsewhere. Show demographics change. Shows splinter off or combine. Crowds move. You need to constantly challenge each show to insure that it is giving you your best value in terms of audience.

Poor staff performance, a different skill set is required to work a show. People attend a tradeshow to do something they do what they cannot do at the office, meet people face-to-face while saving time and expense. Attendees polled reported that when a positive impression was formed about a company 95% of the time it was due to the staff. Conversely when a negative impression was formed 98% of the time it was for the same reason.

You are displaying nothing that is seen as new or compelling. Once seen, things tend to simply become background. This does not mean that you have to introduce a new product or service at every show (people don't buy them anyway - they buy the benefits they derive). You do have to look at new and fresh ways to present them consistent with your core value.

*CEIR

Companies fail to promote before, at or after the event. It borders on criminal to call this "event marketing"; it is really a process. On average 75% of attendees arrive with an agenda in hand. Instead of viewing a show as only a few days, it should be seen as lasting for months. It is a kernel around which a series of cohesive promotional efforts can be built.

An important aspect of this promotion is follow up and the lack of it. Industry surveys have shown that as many as 80% of leads developed on the tradeshow floor are lost in good part to the failure of companies to follow up in a timely fashion. Since your brand is based on a level of confidence in your ability to perform, not fulfilling a simple request for information sends it's own powerful message. It is just not the one you want.

Companies are just ill prepared and the show happens with or without you. Almost invariably the reason why this happens is that there is no commitment on the part of management. Rather than being looked upon as the opportunity to meet and greet the market first hand - show are often viewed as a "necessary evil. "We go because we've always gone, we'd be noticeably absent." Tasks are left on autopilot. The reason behind this lack of commitment and preparedness is the absence of any ROI or ROO mechanism. Mea Culpa.

20% says, the power of the tradeshow is that it compresses time, but this makes the venue equally unforgiving.

Promotions

Promotions refer to a broad range of supporting activities and materials to spur memory or help induce an action on the part of the customer. Some of these inducements include: Coupons, Discounts, Premiums, Incentives, Trial offers, Add-Ons, Contests, Club / Point Systems and others.

Often companies will take the "easy way" and cut price via a coupon drop or discount strategy. While this may have value in encouraging a percentage of new customer acquisition - you have to ask is that the client you want. If their only reason in selecting your product or service is based on price, you will attract a customer list that is principally focused on not spending any money. Frankly if they will jump to you in order to save this month, the likelihood is that they will jump elsewhere next month for the same reason. Good promotions will incorporate other aspects to shift memories of the event to a core value focus. In studies done by Incomm Research, only 20% of promotional materials distributed at a tradeshow actually contributed to increasing memory of the event. How many times have you seen pens, mouse pads and stress balls simply stacked up for attendees to grab as they go past. I have seen promotional materials which were expensive, treated as worthless by the recipients and other goods which were far less costly, received and treated as though they were pure gold. Value is arbitrary and fixed by the customer. The true worth of any promotional product, service or activity is its contribution to the brand and staying power in terms of long term memory. The higher the degree of involvement, the stronger the influence. Inconsistency is your mortal enemy here. Stay in theme to increase the perceived value and promote memorability. Every promotion should contribute to help reinforce your core message.

Packaging

Packaging is sometimes overlooked as a component of the marketing mix. Yet it is sometimes more important than the product. In fact, sometimes the packaging is the product.

The use of packaging inserts is the second highest-ranking method of encouraging customer retention. It is an ideal opportunity to promote directly to someone that already uses your product or service. Inserts such as a coupon to buy more of the same or a piece to educate them as to collateral offerings you have that they would find of interest is in the hands of your highest probable candidate.

Packaging can have it's own significant benefits (and drawbacks). Ask yourself:
Is it easy to open or tamper resistant?
Does it protect the product or showcase it?
Is it informative, interactive or elegant?
Does it enhance and enable use or is it just there to keep all the parts from falling out?
Does it have to be disposed of or does the package have a secondary value in re-use?

Regardless, packaging is an integral part of the overall customer experience. Today fruit juice can be purchased in bottles (either glass or plastic), cans, cups, cartons or, pouches. It can come as single serving sizes or in bulk (gallons, carboys, tanker cars). It can be fresh, frozen or concentrated but it is all fruit juice. The point is that people are buying the use of the product or service in its entirety. (Yes, services are packaged too. Are they a la carte, all inclusive or hybrid bundles?) A package is not a box or a bag, it is a micro-environment. It is the place where your brand lives, until the customer adopts it.

What does your packaging do to add or detract from the experience?

At one point in time I worked with a company in the mid-west that manufactured OEM components. Their products were of a size and weight that allowed the majority of them to be readily shipped individually via carriers such as UPS or Federal Express. To avoid breakage, they used a heavy weight carton and a foam-in-place system. Bulk shipments consisted of individual boxes bound on skids. For years that worked very well. They began to find increasing sales resistance in Europe, not because of the product but due to the packaging. Disposal costs were dramatically higher there and the foam packing could not be recycled. They changed to a palletainer pack for bulk shipments and found that not only were their European clients happier, their large domestic accounts were too. They began saving on disposal and storage costs. On top of everything else, the bulk containers cost less.

20% says packaging can and should carry more than just the product - it carries the message.

Public Relations

You <u>are</u> news. Here is an opportunity to deliver your message in a format that provides an independent third party endorsement. It is an excellent way to build your image in a partnership with your industry media including:

- Editorial content
- Press releases
- Contests
- Awards
- Feature articles
- Press conferences
- Public service or awareness

Public relations is not "free advertising", because it is not free. There is always a cost to everything. True you are not paying for the print space or airtime, but you are paying in the investment you must make to court the press coverage and prepare materials properly for acceptance.

It is all about relationships...

The "product" of the media - is news. Press releases are in essence then, "free product". It would be nice if it were that simple but the reality is that it is like going to a buffet. You don't start indiscriminately consuming everything from one end of the table to the other. You pick and choose, old favorites and new things that look interesting. This is no different.

I am reminded of a story about George Bernard Shaw. A young man had asked him how best to go about getting published. In his typical fashion Shaw advised him to go down to the publisher and wait.

The play write said, one morning the publisher will come out and ask if there is anything new from Shaw and be told no. Then he will say, all right - time to start on the garbage. That is your chance.

Editors are inundated with press releases vying for their attention. They do what you would naturally expect. They give an ear to the people who bring them advertising dollars or prestige. They look at sources where they have relationships, people that have brought them good stories in the past. They look at material that catches their eye, fills a timely need and is in a format that works. Editorial calendars are published long in advance. You may have an exciting new software package, but if the magazine is featuring chemical products that month you stand a good chance of being overlooked. After four months of a poor editorial fit, when they are focusing on software, you may be passed over once more because they seen your piece time and again they consider it "old news". You must maintain periodic contact with editors to stay "in front" with your story.

DO NOT call a press conference if you can tell your story in any other fashion. They are costly both in time and money. If the press attends and does not see the value, you will alienate a powerful ally.

20% says - all the other rules of marketing also apply to marketing your press release too.

Press releases & Media kits

Press release should be constructed in an inverted pyramid style. Although your goal is commercial, this is still a "news story" and has to follow that format. Avoid editorializing, stick to the facts. Don't make unsupported claims; use quotes instead to include opinions. "Jack Jones, VP of Engineering said that...". Include contact information and resist the temptation to "sell". First and foremost, if it is not newsworthy, you are wasting your time and alienating the people you want most on your side by wasting their time. Use the "inverted pyramid" format for lay out.

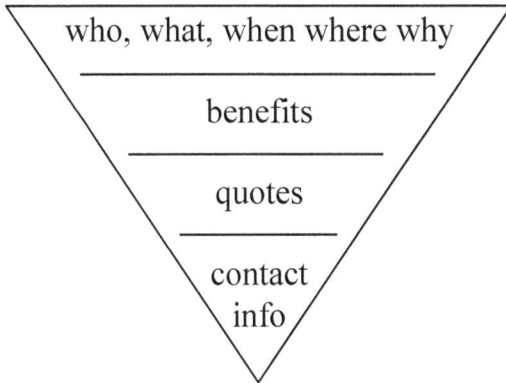

A good headline will do more to help sell the piece than anything else will. Keep your media kits simple so that the editors do not have to hunt for the story. They can be electronic or hard copy but familiarize yourself with acceptable formats to make your story easy to choose and use. High quality photographs with well-written captions are a big plus.

Public relations by itself can be a full time job. Do it or not, but a half-hearted effort is not something to send to the press.

"You can make more friends in two months by becoming interested in other people than you can in two years by trying to get other people interested in you."

Dale Carnegie

Section 8 - CRM Systems...

Does CRM stand for customer relationship _management_ or _misconceptions_?

Good news - you already have one.
Bad news - you already have one.

On the subject of acquisition and retention, I should sell a bumper sticker that says, "customer attrition happens". It occurs naturally through our own actions and inactions. While it is possible, it is very unusual that a change takes place without some indication of what is going on. In reality we are not watching. We want to believe that we are doing a good job and so we only look for those clues that support that hypothesis. It is human nature. After all, looking for our shortcomings is tantamount to an admission we are under-performing. So we turn a blind eye. Just like the old sayings - No news is good news, Don't rock the boat and of course, Just ignore them - they will go away.

People retire or move on. Projects are started or cancelled. Companies are bought and sold. Departments are formed and merged. Will you be ready?

Nothing happens in a vacuum. As relationships are better built and managed, the more you understand what dynamics are shaping the process. When some one retires or transfers, you know who the successor will be. Before a project is placed on hold or cancelled outright, contacts in other areas might be helping to guide you as to where those resources have been re-allocated but only if you have taken the time to develop them.

It costs far less to market deeper through an existing client that it does to continually cultivate new ones. You are already a known entity. You have already established a basis for trust.

When Dell Computer first committed to their on-line strategy, they hoped to generate $50,000,000 a year in sales through their web portal. Today their daily volume is close to that number. Why? Other people (in fact lots of other people) sell computers and peripherals on-line. Many of them sell these items for less money than Dell. The answer is simple; they are viewed as vendors of commodities. <u>Dell is not because Dell did not sell computers.</u> Dell sought out their best client base, first in industry and education because they had large networks to administrate. Then they looked at where core challenges existed that they were able to address within their core capabilities. What they found was that networks were challenged by the inconsistency of their parts. Hardware and software acquired at different times from multiple sources were creating a nightmare. LAN administrators were pulling their hair out just trying to keep everything talking to each other. Countless hours and millions of dollars were being invested every year to try and keep these patchwork systems functioning in a world where the moving target of technology would alter the equation almost daily.

20% says the difference between a problem and an opportunity is the right solution.

The real problem was too many choices. The logical solution was to narrow them down. Here is the approved hardware with the necessary software already installed, price based on your aggregate purchasing volume and available through your own dedicated portal.

Dell built computers but what they sold was the absence of network conflicts and purchasing problems. Their success in the home user market was a natural extension. Customers, who have a good experience with their product and service at the office, take it home with them when they need a new system.

Look at 20% functioning here. Identifying the ideal customer, adhering to core values and capabilities, isolating the root cause of the problem and presenting a simple, repeatable solution. The customer relation management system is built around that kind of understanding and appreciation of the client's needs. Most CRM systems fail because they are not CRM systems.

Its not about software, its not about hardware,
It's about where your head is at...
If it doesn't work on paper, it won't work even faster on a computer.

Error # 1 - The purpose of a CRM system is not just to sell more stuff. It's about understanding what the customer needs so that you can position as a problem solver. People implement an information management system and mistakenly think that they have a CRM. Instead of matching preferences and offerings, they begin sending the customer everything they sell in hopes that they hit pay dirt.

Error # 2 - You eat a whale one bite at a time, don't try to implement a CRM system globally. Use incremental stages to work out the bugs, approaching the highest value (20% rule) first. Take time to build templates and establish clear-cut procedures so that during the course of implementation you do not have people creating and instituting their own "solutions" to fill in gaps.

Error # 3 - Remember it is just a tool, not a cure-all. Establish goals, timelines and milestones for success up-front. Gauge your progress regularly and build feedback loops into the process to ascertain how and where the program is contributing to the customer's experience.

Error # 4 - Do not let your focus be diverted. Name a single champion (someone with patience) and empower them to shepherd the project.

Error # 5 - An important part of error #4 is to avoid unreasonable expectations. This is a very long-range commitment and full benefit derives from an attitude shift to a spirit of partnering with your customers. This is not something that you can or should expect to recognize an immediate return.

Error # 6 - Decide how much is too much. Define the extent of relationship you need to succeed. Information has an addictive property and like any addiction, our need to satisfy it grows insidiously. Establish guidelines as to what is and what is not relevant.

A CRM system is really about seeking creative solutions.

It's about re-focusing your energy to serve rather than sell.

It's about creating an environment where the client is more anxious to buy than you are to sell.

Since 72% of all purchases are buyer initiated, isn't that a better place to be.

APPENDIX

20% RE-CAP

- 20% marketing is about positioning your company as the first, best option from the customer's perspective.

- Establish clear cut, timely, measurable goals.

- Develop a thorough understanding of your own core capabilities to supply consistent, appropriate solutions.

- Based on your culture and capabilities, identify who your ideal client base is.

- Understand the unfulfilled needs of the customer or prospect from their perspective.

- What are the root causes for these needs.

- Exactly how do you answer these needs, in terms that the customer will embrace?

- Boil that message down into a clear hierarchy that conveys the key benefits as rapidly as possible.

- No more than three benefits at a time.

- Map multiple paths to deliver that message to your client base.

- Listen. Have a feedback loop in place. Look for trends.

- A brand is really a promise, underwritten by the trust that your customer places in your ability to perform.

- Everybody has a brand - most people simply fail to capitalize on it.

- The four elements of the brand are clarity, consistency, repetition and change.

- You cannot be all things to all people, but you can be the best thing to some people.

- It is far easier and more profitable to retain and increase business with an existing client than to continuously find new ones.

- Your biggest competitor is the unreasonable expectation you set in the customer's mind - because you can never live up to it.

- Timing varies, personal preferences vary, you need a solid mix to deliver your message where and when the client is ready to hear it.

- Everything makes a difference either positive or negative - there is no neutral ground.

- The most expensive promotion, advertisement, tradeshow, mailing or program you can undertake is the one that fails to meet its objectives - or worse - one that works contrary to your goals.

THE GOLDEN RULES
OF
20 PERCENT MARKETING

20 Percent Marketing is all about establishing and maintaining relationships.

Every sound relationship is based on trust and respect.

Trust and respect are earned based on performance.

Your performance is based on setting and meeting expectations every time.

Setting appropriate expectations can only happen by understanding your core capabilities and values. Without that, you cannot maintain repeatable, profitable performance.

Every sound relationship works for the common interests of all parties.

Reference Sources:

Cahners
CEIR (Center for Exhibit Industry Research)
Creative Good
Digital Impact
DMA (Direct Marketers Association)
eMarketer Magazine
Ernst & Young
Exhibit Surveys
Incomm Research
IMT
Jupiter Research
Peppers & Rogers
Primus
Veronis & Suhler
US Census Bureau

Some Recommended or Referenced Authors

Harry Beckwith
Dale Carnegie
Stephen Covey
Napoleon Hill
Richard Koch
John Naisbitt
Peppers & Rogers
Jack Trout
Sergio Zyman

About the Author

20 Percent Marketing is the second business book by Paul Holland. His first book on marketing *Hobert Does a Trade Show*, which he both wrote and illustrated is an amusing yet serious overview of the trade show and event world.

He is an accomplished speaker on a number of subjects and has authored works of fiction as well including one short novel and collected short stories.

He has designed over 200 products and product improvements and worked in numerous different industries including biotechnology, environmental, event marketing and fluidics...

He currently resides in New Jersey with his wife and best friend, Rosie in a house that he designed and built himself.

They consider their three children their greatest accomplishment.

www.ingramcontent.com/pod-product-compliance
Lightning Source LLC
Chambersburg PA
CBHW060038210326
41520CB00009B/1173